READERS PRAISE for NEVER SATISFIED

"Not one line was wasted. Every sentence, paragraph, and chapter was intense and educational. No one should be without this thought provoking piece of literature."
Lisa Smith, School Teacher
New York, NY

"It's about time someone came along to explain cheating from the man's perspective. The truth may be out, but at least it doesn't point the finger only at the men."
James Adams, Auto Mechanic
Los Angeles, CA

"I'm going to buy a copy of this book for my stupid girlfriends who are dealing with married men. If they won't listen to me tell them it's a waste of time, maybe they will listen to the truth from the mouth of a man."
Rebecca Williams, Hair Stylist
Nashville, TN

"NEVER SATISFIED is the most realistic and honest portrayal of infidelity I've ever read. Michael doesn't attempt to preach and point fingers, only to enlighten and raise consciousness. I don't know whether to punch him out or shake his hand, but I will definitely buy the book."
Eddie Robinson, Construction Worker
New Orleans, LA

"The chapter title, *No More Mr. Nice Guy*, made me feel redeemed. For the very first time I felt like someone really understood my frustration and distrust towards women. Hopefully some of them will read this book and stop playing games. Thanks Michael for airing out the dirty laundry."

Gerald Young, Store Manager
Detroit, MI

"INTERESTING, INTELLIGENT, AND FUNNY AS HELL. Michael did an excellent job of bringing his characters to life. I felt their anxiety and could see the shocking expressions on their faces. But what he does best is draw you into the stories. One minute I was slamming my fist on the table in rage, and one paragraph later I was laughing my butt off. What an emotional rollercoaster. I hope to hear from him again very soon with another wonderful piece of work. Bravo, and Congratulations!"

Deidra Harris, Systems Analysis
Atlanta, GA

"NEVER SATISFIED will shoot straight to the top of the best seller list and become the 90s bible for male infidelity. Women will love it because of the eye-opening details, and men will appreciate its frankness. What's even more impressive is the way in which Michael communicates his message of integrity in a universal language. Whether you are young, or old, rich, or poor, black, or white this book speaks to you. Personally I was most overwhelmed by the bold story telling. After reading one page I thought it was interesting. But after reading one chapter, I knew it was going to be something very special!!!"

Cheryl Fitzpatrick, Lawyer
Chicago, IL

NEVER SATISFIED
How & Why Men Cheat

NEVER SATISFIED

How & Why Men Cheat

BY MICHAEL BAISDEN

Seventh Printing 2001

Cover Design by Latanya Davis
Creative Glue, Atlanta, Georgia

Legacy Publishing
P.O. Box 6555
Katy, TX 77491-6555

Library of Congress Catalog No: 94-096628
ISBN: 0-9643675-8-0

Printed in the United States of America

To Michae', my daughter, and my inspiration.
Although you may only be three years old now, hopefully
you will one day benefit from what daddy had to say.

I love you, sweetheart.

CONTENTS

ACKNOWLEDGEMENTS

There are so many people to thank, I don't know where to begin. My partners Sam Jones, Mandell Wooden, and Rodney Julun were very supportive during the 14 long months it took to write this book. They never doubted that I could do it, nor did they interrupt my late night writing binges. But most importantly, I'd like to thank them for not tempting me to go out when the clubs were jumpin' and the weather outside was absolutely beautiful. I'm also indebted to my co-workers Ben Benton, Eugene Taylor, Rolland King, Adrienne Brown, and Mr. Harris for all their encouragement. I went through several periods of writers block, but their kind words helped me get over it and back to work. I must also thank the thousands of CTA train passengers who put up with me nagging them to read the manuscript on the train. I know they're glad it's over and they can finally read the book without my looking over their shoulders to make corrections.

To my best friend Lois Baisden, who kept me from starving to death while writing, I'd like to say "Thank You." I could always count on you to be there for me when I needed someone to talk to. Last but not least, I'd like to thank my dear mother Alicia Parham. Not only did she support me financially with this and other business ventures, but she did one hell of a job raising three kids on her own. You'll always be my number one girl. I love you more than words can say.

INTRODUCTION

I realize this book may initially ignite feelings of betrayal by my male peers. My close associates asked me "Why would you expose all of our 'male' secrets?" Never fear, men, I have not sold out to the ever-multiplying, verbally-castrating, talk show hosts who have seemingly conspired to use the male ego as a doormat. What I am attempting to do, at the very least, is to expose the games that are quite seriously destroying our relationships with our women, and, as a direct result, affecting our ability to maintain healthy relationships which could be beneficial to both ourselves and the children that are unsuspecting players in too many of those very games.

During my research, I found it rather interesting that whenever the subject of male infidelity was addressed, there was an apparent absence of anyone representing the attitude of today's man. The usual assortment of angry female authors and sexually repressed suburban Ph.d's were always in attendance, but who wants to hear those tired perspectives all over again? Not the frustrated woman of the 90's, that's for sure. She is sick and tired of pointless bickering and scientific theories. Just try explaining to any sane woman that the reason she found her husband in bed, buck naked, with her best friend was because of a problem he experienced as a child that has affected his ability to make a commitment. I would now suggest that you get the hell out of striking distance. The possibility of getting cursed out is also a very good bet. I'm not discounting the legitimacy of studies regarding infidelity, but the time has come for a more comprehensive and up to date point of view. One that is truly reflective of what really goes on behind closed doors and between the sheets.

Now let's deal with the ever popular "Dog Theory" which contends that all men who cheat are dogs. This cliche has become the rallying cry for every woman who has ever been cheated on, lied to, knocked up, put out, or maybe simply wasn't offered a seat on the bus. Although this may be a very catchy topic for the morning television talk shows, it doesn't seriously address the problem. By submitting to the notion that "Boys will be boys" or as some women so eloquently put it, "Dogs will be dogs," you are only validating the irresponsible behavior of men. Don't accept this conduct as a simple case of males acting out their manhood. Men cheat for the same reasons that women do, they choose to.

Another reason why I explicitly discourage this type of language is because it is biased. It singles out the man and subjugates him to the status of animal, which innately puts women on a pedestal above men with regards to behavior and morals. But who are these accommodating creatures the so-called "Dogs" are cheating with? What about them? Does the term "She Dog" seem befitting? Men must unquestionably be accountable for their devious conduct, but simply calling them dogs does not speak to the many circumstances involving their infidelity. If you still insist your man is a dog, I suggest you get rid of him and find a real man. He may be more expensive to feed, but at least he won't come home with fleas.

One of the distinct differences between this book and others which have dealt with this subject, is the inclusion of explicit details regarding how men cheat. How many times have you thought to yourself "If only I could read his mind." Well, how about the next best thing? Sitting in on a group of men engaged in a candid discussion about every intimate detail of their sordid affairs. Now, tell me that doesn't make your mouth water? What I believe women will find most interesting is not the specific details of the information, but the degree of conceit which these men exhibited while sharing their so-called methods of cheating.

The ultimate question, however, is not if men will continue to play these games, but whether or not women will ever identify and confront their own ignorance and tolerance for allowing it to continue.

Let the games begin!

CHAPTER 1
TRICKS OF THE TRADE

What methods will a man utilize to conceal his affair? And how many lies will he tell to maintain these sordid relationships? These tricks, or *games* as women refer to them, have been the reasons behind many break-ups and divorces. It seems technology has made the game of cheating much simpler to play with the innovation of pagers, car phones, etc. But regardless of scientific advances, one simple fact remains, a man must forever keep his lies straight, because with one slip of the tongue, his world could come tumbling down around him.

THE HUNT

Any successful hunt must begin with the selection of the ideal geographic location to find a particular animal. The cheating man understands this fact and has carefully considered where he will lay his insidious traps. The most commonly preferred places are the bars, night clubs, and lounges. These modern day meat markets provide the perfect stalking grounds for any man with the desire to "temporarily resign" from his existing relationship. Nowhere else can such an alluring combination of women, alcohol, and immorality be found under one roof. He feels right at home in this perverse jungle where cordial admiration is but visual assault, and the art of good conversation has been degenerated to nothing more than a prerequisite to sex.

Considering that those women who frequent these establishments are fully aware of the unsavory characteristics of night life, one might wonder, "Why do they continually go back for more?" Well, men have formulated their own ideas. They believe these women are either desperately lonely, extremely bored, or simply hard up. Are they right? Most women would probably say no, but actions speak louder than words. Every weekend they pile inside over crowded clubs wearing tight skirts, heavy make up, and way too much perfume. Their piercing stares and suggestive body language declares, "Tonight is the night." There is no doubt many of these women, while not openly admitting it, are romantically entertaining thoughts of finding that special man, *Mr. Right*. Unfortunately, this obscure fantasy plays right into the hands of the hunter who will most certainly use it as another weapon to get what he wants, uncommitted sex.

Some women do eventually wake up and realize the club is no place to meet a decent man. After years of putting up with the exhausting and childish games associated with night life, they grab their coats and purses vowing never to return. However, this rude awakening is of no concern to the hunter, who is confident that next week will bring countless others to take their places. They will be lined up halfway around the block in the cold and rain, desperately waiting to get into the club, like lambs being led to slaughter. And it is from amongst these unsuspecting creatures that the next "other woman" will be chosen. Who will it be, and why?

The attitude of many women is, "Men will lay down with anything with a heartbeat." That indictment may well be valid if the cheating man is only interested in a one night stand. However, if he intends on maintaining an ongoing affair, specific requirements must be met, one of which is Empathy. The other woman must be willing to accept his current relationship without "rocking the boat." Most cheating men, especially the married ones, will come right out and tell her the details of his situation. This will allow her to make a judgment as to whether or not she can go along with the program. Respect and consideration for his wife or girlfriend is absolutely necessary if the relationship has any chance at longevity. <u>Sexual inhibition</u> is another of these prerequisites. If the other woman won't allow him to be sexually adventurous, then what the hell does he need her for? He can be bored at home. Men have the idea in mind that when they find this other woman, she will be perfectly willing to do all those things he was too afraid or uncomfortable to ask from his wife or girlfriend. This includes doing the wild thing in raunchy places.

<u>Loyalty</u> is also an important attribute. The cheating man, despite his own infidelity, needs a woman whom he can trust not to "Run The Streets." If he calls at 12:00 midnight on a Saturday night, she had better be there. He doesn't want to hear any nonsense about her going out with girlfriends. In his mind, she is his personal sex slave who must make herself available 24 hours a day. As the relationship develops, she is restricted from pursuing other intimate associations, and is expected to be completely loyal to him. Any breach of this unwritten contract will prompt him to terminate the affair and go hunting elsewhere. Women see this as extremely hypocritical since he himself is cheating.

<u>Physical Beauty</u> would have to be the least most important attribute. Don't get me wrong, I'm not implying that men who cheat are only interested in ugly women. What I am merely saying is, a woman who is exceptionally attractive and terrible in bed is not all that valuable an asset to the cheating man. He would prefer a woman of moderate looks with a firm body who will screw his brains out on a consistent basis (understand my point?).

The process of choosing this qualified woman from out of the crowd is a complex one. As you well know, the night club is a very *dense* place. Therefore, the hunter must keep his eyes sharp, and position himself in the areas where his efforts can be maximized. Often you will notice him sitting at the bar, standing by the door, or looking down over the crowd from atop his perch. He wants to be the first to move in for the kill if a vulnerable woman should arrive, or should I say, a wounded animal? Once he spots his target, the chase is on. Armed with a fresh hair cut, splash of cologne, and hopefully a breath mint, he sets out on his lustful safari.

Just as the animal hunter relies on guns, traps, and camouflage to capture his prey, the cheating man depends on smooth talk, good looks, and the low morals of his victims to accomplish his goals. But determining whether a particular woman has the characteristics which will suit his purpose is not such an easy task in the night club environment. Loud music, incurable perpetrating, and the woman's nosy girlfriends make the process all the more difficult. This leaves him with little else to go on except a woman's attire. More precisely, what she's wearing and how she's wearing it. This is the first indication as to her level of availability, class, and morality. But due to the fact that short, tight miniskirts are commonplace wherever you go, the perception is that most of the women in the club are dizzy, promiscuous whores looking for action.

This hasty assumption has been the cause of many heated verbal exchanges. The hunter, who is only out for sex, cannot or will not distinguish between the hoochies and the respectable women who are simply out for fun. From his perspective, the woman wearing the revealing outfit which shows off her "tangible assets" is sending a specific message, "I am available and want to be approached." And then again, some men may perceive it as a invitation to touch, grasp and be disrespectful. There is no doubt many women expect these types of impulses since they go to such great lengths to expose so much of themselves. They are shamelessly sending a message regarding their availability, while adamantly demanding to be acknowledged. The hunter is merely reimbursing her for her troubles.

On the other hand, the woman who elects to dress conservatively is viewed as more ethical and self-assured. The message she sends is, "I'm confident enough in what I am wearing to attract a man who is about something." Some men also perceive her as more intelligent, trustworthy, and loyal. However, on more than a few occasions men have admitted to being fooled. The seductively dressed woman has been found to be very laid back. While the woman who was seemingly conservative turned out to be wild and loose, or as some would say, "A Super Freak." After making a thorough survey of his domain, the hunter will likely play the odds and pursue the woman dressed like a skeezzer. After all, he's not looking for a lifelong wife to take home to mamma, only a part time whore to take home to bed.

Clearly, the night club is nothing more than a weekly production specifically designed for play, profit, and perpetrating. The music is loud, the drinks are expensive, and everyone is dressed up in their Sunday best. On this pretentious stage nothing is what it appears to be. When the doors open, the curtain goes up and it's show time. Unemployed men suddenly become corporate executives, and women on welfare masquerade as fashion models. With all the role playing and B.S. going on, it's no wonder why women perpetually complain about not being able to find a good man at the club. Hell, even a so-called good man will step out to briefly forget just how good he is. However, not all men seek their mistresses and lovers at these "night spots." Most prefer surroundings that are more comfortable and familiar. A place where they can mix business with pleasure.

While the night time may be the right time, the daytime has become prime time, for fooling around that is. The workplace has become the "hot spot" for infidelity in the 90's. Women are on the job in record numbers, occupying every position from secretary to C. E. O. This reality puts men and women in direct contact with one another on a daily basis. In the morning they board crowded buses and trains together. And for eight long hours they work in cramped office spaces, brushing up against one another by accident and by choice. It was only a matter of time before the fireworks began. A cordial invitation to have a quick lunch passionately erupts into an *indecent* proposal to have a quickie for lunch. All the while, the hunter is getting paid.

There should be no mystery as to why extramarital affairs are flourishing on the J-O-B. It is the ideal place for the cheating man to meet a woman who is compatible, desirable, and equally as important, employed. And unlike the club scene, the workplace allows for a more gradual progression towards intimacy; there is no rush. In this environment the hunter appears more like a scavenger, leisurely waiting for the slow death of an existing relationship so he can swoop down like a vulture and pick up the scraps of the emotionally torn victim. He is a great listener too, especially if it's a derogatory story about the woman's terrible husband or boyfriend. The reliable shoulder to cry on, he is often the man women look to for support, never realizing, however, the support he really wants to give is in the form of his penis.

Workplace affairs are mutually pursued involvements where both parties are generally up front about their marital status and living arrangements. The woman explains that she is not seriously involved, and the man swears his existing relationship is on the rocks. However, one of them is lying. Can you guess which one it is? That's right, the conniving hunter. He knows that honesty isn't always the best policy when it comes to capturing his prey. He prefers to bend the truth a bit until he has the woman's heart firmly secured in his trap. After that, he can utilize his subversive skills to maintain her ignorance and trust. In other words, he will continue to lie his ass off to keep her from finding him out. The trick, men say, is to communicate the status of their relationships in such a way as to leave room for diplomacy.

How many times have you heard the ever popular, "My woman and I are having problems?" Or "My wife is married but I'm not?" And if all else fails, he'll give her his best line, "I'm getting a divorce," when he knows damn well he's not going anywhere with three kids to support and a mortgage to pay. The real question is, do women really fall for these tired lines? Or do they simply accept them in order to justify the relationship in their own minds? The cheating man doesn't care one way or the other. His only objective is to relax her defenses long enough to reel her in emotionally. Any lie will do.

Men who elect to tell these lies about being miserable at home must continue to show signs of their unhappiness. Now the game becomes more difficult to play and the likelihood of getting busted increases. The wife or girlfriend begins to notice a sudden change in his attitude and his routine. First he starts showing up late from work. "I had to work an extra shift, baby," he'll say. But his overtime is not limited to filling out paperwork, I assure you. Then he'll discourage her from visiting him on the job. No doubt to avoid running into his *work whore*. Finally, the most obvious sign of infidelity, his wedding ring, abruptly *disappears*. Of course, he'll try to use the lame excuse of, "I lost it." When that doesn't work, the next step is to merely find a reason to leave it at home altogether. Men are notorious for using their work as a reason for taking off their bands. "It's interfering with my ability to do my job," he says. Now, that excuse may not be much of a lie, since his new job is chasing pussy.

Eventually the hunter will capture his prey, either at the club or on the job. The next task is to find a way to communicate with his new found lover without being detected. Now the real games begin.

CALL ME

"Communication is the key to any successful relationship." This is the claim of therapists and marriage counselors everywhere. The cheating man absolutely agrees with this theory, particularly where communicating with the other woman is concerned. Some men have elevated this phase of cheating to an art form, while others are so clumsy and indiscreet, you suspect their wives and girlfriends are deaf, dumb, and blind. Regardless of what the man's level of sophistication is, the technology of today has made it quite simple to reach out and touch someone. One innovation that has revolutionized infidelity is the portable pager. For many men this has been the best invention since the TV remote control. And you know how important a scientific breakthrough that was. The pager is a small device which can be easily carried and is simple to operate. Best of all, it provides the man with a reliable and inexpensive means of communication between himself and a prospective lover. It may not be as legitimate as a home number, but he's not exactly involved in a legitimate game, now is he?

Pagers come in a wide variety of styles with a number of different features. Services such as voice mail, alpha numeric pagers, and sky pager networks have lifted the vintage act of cheating out of the stone age and into the 20th century. There is also an optional vibrator selector, not to be confused with the vibrator recommended by Dr. Ruth, which allows the user to receive pages silently by causing the pager to pulsate. These numerous alternatives provide men with all the technological advantages they will need to carry out their conspiracy of deception and trickery.

However, the creation of technical gadgets does not automatically guarantee that every man is gifted with the same level of ability to effectively use them. What I'm trying to say is, some men couldn't trick their way out of a paper bag. One of those unsuccessful cheating men is 29–year–old Mark. During the last six months of his marriage, he's already been busted twice trying to stay in touch with his mistress. Which is a bit excessive considering he's only been married eight months. He honestly admits that cheating is not exactly his forte. In his words, "Some people can get away with murder, but I would probably get arrested for stealing a stick of bubble gum." Nevertheless, he kept on trying until finally his novice tricks left him open yet again.

Like most men who rush off to the altar, I never considered how much my life would be changed by simply saying, "I do." First of all, I could no longer hang out with the boys all night. Secondly, I had to put up with hair all over the sink, and tampon wrappers in the waste basket. And then there was the ultimate sacrifice, not being able to give my home number out to different women. Back in the good old days when I was single, my telephone would ring off the hook. Sometimes the answering machine tape would run out because of the large numbers of incoming calls. But after walking down the aisle with Erica, the only calls I got were from boring family members, annoying telemarketers, and aggressive bill collectors. This went on for the first three months of our marriage before I decided something had to be done. And I knew just the person to call for advice.

My best friend Randy is a real ladies man. I guess you could say he has a black belt in the art of cheating. Throughout my engagement he begged and pleaded with me not to go through with it. But my mind was made up. I was hopelessly in love and thoroughly pussy whipped. Anyway, I called him at home the minute Erica walked out the door to go grocery shopping. As the phone rang, I prepared myself for the usual verbal abuse. Randy hated the idea of my being married and reminded me of it every chance he got. This time would be no different.

"Hello Randy, this is Mark, what's up?"

"Well, well, well, if it isn't Mr. Hen Pecked Husband himself."

"Ha Ha, very funny. Look, before you start going off, I've got a serious situation over here and I need your help."

"In that case partner, you've got my undivided attention," he said sounding concerned. "What exactly is the problem?"

"Well, the problem is that I haven't been able to receive any calls in privacy in months. Erica is always at home and she rushes to answer the phone every time it rings."

"I told you not to marry Ms. Nosybody," he interrupted. "Why do you think I hardly ever call? She monitors your conversations like a goddamn prison guard."

"Hold on Randy, I didn't call so you could crack on my wife. All I wanted was a few tips."

"I'm sorry Mark, but I hate to see a good man go down."

"I may be down but I'm not out. Which brings me back to the point of this phone call. How can I keep in touch with my other women without Erica finding out?"

"Ok rookie, break out your pencil and paper. The master is going to take you to school. Step number one, have them call when Erica is at work. Don't you work the midnight shift?"

"Yeah."

"Perfect!" he shouted. "Just arrange your calls between 9:00 am and 5:00 pm."

"I already tried that trick, you idiot."

"And, what happened?"

"I got busted, that's what. Erica came home for lunch one day and the phone was ringing off the hook. I tried to play it off but she knew what was up. After that incident, she began showing up unannounced two or three times a week. And sometimes she would even take the entire day off without any advance notice."

"Ok then, let's move on to step number two, the one ring signal."

"The one ring signal, huh? How does that work?"

"Suppose you have plans to see your mistress but you want to make sure everything is still set. What you do is have her call your house, let the phone ring once, then hang up, get it?"

"Oh, I'll get it alright, a good ass kicking from Erica if I try to pull that dumb trick. Is that the best you can come up with?"

"Look homie, what you really need to do is stop acting like a poor pimp and get yourself a beeper."

"Are you out of your mind? Erica hates those things. She says men who wear them look like drug dealers."

"Mark, this is 1994. Everybody and their momma has a pager. And who says she has to know anyway?"

As much as I hated to admit it, he was right. The only way to play in the big league was to have some means of communication. So, the very next morning I drove down to the beeper store and had my service activated. They even threw in a stack of those cheap business cards to sweeten the deal. I felt like a real international playboy ready to conquer the world.

It didn't take long to get use to the idea of having a pager. I gave my number out to every woman who even so much as looked cross-eyed at me, a total of at least 20 during the first month. Some of them asked if I was married, some didn't. As far as I was concerned, it wasn't any of their damned business. My attitude was, "Either you want the number or you don't." And besides, my marital status should have been apparent anyway. I mean really ladies, if a man says he wants to get to know you better and then refuses to give out his home number, that should tell you something, right? If that's not obvious enough, what about those fresh tan marks on his ring finger? A woman would have to be as blind as Ray Charles to miss that one. As I was saying, my love life was booming. Women were beeping me every 30 minutes. You would've thought I was giving away money. "I've got to slow down," I warned myself. "Erica isn't stupid, she's going to notice the change in my routine." But what I was really concerned most about was slipping up. Cheating wasn't exactly my field of expertise.

Two months and God knows how many women later, the pager was working out perfectly. The most difficult part was keeping it out of Erica's sight. One of my best hiding places was inside the glove compartment of my old beat up Buick. She hated that car with a passion and wouldn't be caught dead riding or even sitting in it. And on the rare occasions when I had to bring it into the house, I simply placed the selector switch on vibrate, wrapped it inside a smelly gym sock, and stuffed it in the bottom of the drawer. No woman in her right mind would go within 50 feet of one of my socks, let me tell you. But even after taking all of these precautions, it seemed inevitable that I would become careless, which is exactly what happened six months to the day of our wedding.

I remember that day like it was yesterday. It was a Friday and the weather was cloudy. Erica wanted to make a big deal out of being married for 6 months by having a candlelight dinner and bottle of wine. You know how sentimental women can be, they want to celebrate every occasion from their first kiss to losing their virginity. I agreed to go along with all the hoopla under one condition, that I be allowed to go to the gym before we got all romantic and mushy. She gave in to my request and by 5:30 pm I was out the door, headed for the gym and the nearest pay phone. I figured, why not kill two birds with one stone? When I pulled my pager from out of the glove compartment, there were four calls. I returned the two important ones, and erased the others. Afterwards, I went to the gym as promised, to work up an appetite for Erica's great cooking.

By 7:00 I was exhausted from playing basketball and lifting weights. I took a quick shower, put on a fresh pair of drawers, and started towards home. The minute I drove up to the apartment, I could smell the pot roast baking in the oven. My stomach was growling so loud I thought it was going to set off my neighbors car alarm. We lived on the fifth floor, but it only took me five seconds to run up the stairs. When I walked in the door, Erica had dinner all laid out on the table. I quickly washed my hands, said an abbreviated prayer, and commenced to stuffing myself like a pig.

After dinner, Erica quickly put away the dishes and joined me on the sofa where I had collapsed from indigestion. We sat there cuddled up like teenagers watching television until 10:00, that's when I brushed up against the arm of the sofa and felt my pager clipped to my belt. In my hurry to feed my face, I had forgotten to leave it in the car. I had to think fast.

"Excuse me for a second baby, lift up so I can scratch my side."

"Oh no you don't," she said playfully. "This is as comfortable as I've been in a long time. Just lift up your sweater and I'll reach around and scratch it for you."

"That's quite alright honey! Just stay where you are, I'll get it."

I calmly reached underneath my sweater to make sure it was in the off position. Just as I managed to get my finger on the switch, guess what happened. That's right, I received a page.

"Oh shit," I thought. "Who in the world is calling me this late at night?"

Luckily, the selector switch was in the vibrator position so I figured she wouldn't notice the humming sound or feel the pulsating. But in an awkward situation such as this, a trembling pager feels more like a major earthquake, especially after you've put in a fresh pack of Energizer batteries. Needless to say, the gig was up.

"What in the hell is that?" she asked as she lifted from my lap.

"What are you talking about, baby?" I replied, looking guilty as can be.

"Don't play games with me, Mark. Are you wearing a pager?"

"Let me explain, sweetheart. I'm holding it for one of

the guys at the gym. He's going out of town and asked me to respond to his business calls."

"You must think I'm a damned fool or something. Do you honestly expect me to believe that?"

"Yes I do!" I shouted as if I was telling the truth. "When he gets back you can ask him yourself."

"I've got a better idea," she said with her hands on her hips. "Why don't we just call back the number on the pager and see who it is. I'll get on the phone in the bedroom, and you can answer your buddy's *business* call. How about that?"

(Gulp) I took a hard swallow and apprehensively went to get the phone while she followed close behind to make sure I dialed in the correct number. I was busted and we both knew it. There was no way in hell I was going to call back that number, and I didn't. So, she grabbed the pager out of my hand and dialed the number herself. When the phone picked up, she cursed the woman out so bad I had to leave the room. Afterwards she cursed me out too and then packed up her things and went to her mother for the rest of the weekend. Since that incident took place, her whole family has been talking about me like a dog. Even her brother, who is a big time cheater himself, had the nerve to curse me out. He said, "Any man who is stupid enough to get caught doing some dumb shit like that deserves to be treated like a dog." Maybe he has a point. Oh well, back to the drawing board.

Unlike the novice, the sophisticated cheating man knows exactly how to optimize the use of all of his resources, even a device as simple as a pager. The James Bond type, as I call him, will have a system of codes more elaborate than the C. I. A. He has to protect himself against the possibility of his woman recovering numbers or messages from his pager. When the other woman pages him, he will simply explain the odd numbers as a "technical malfunction." Numbers like 1000, 111, and 911 appear all too often. But these crude numbers have precise meaning for Mr. Bond, you can bet. He knows that 1000 means "Meet me at 10:00 pm, you know where." The place to rendezvous has already been prearranged. All it takes is a quick page to verify she has made it safely to the motel. 111 means "I could not find a babysitter. We'll have to try again for tomorrow night." Now he can stop looking so damned nervous about which lie he had planned to tell to get out of the house, at least for tonight. 911 of course, is the code for emergency. What this basically signals is that the other woman doesn't give a damn how busy he is. She expects him to drop whatever he's doing and call her back *immediately*. Usually, the only emergency is the fire she needs put out in her pants.

Another clever method of communicating with the other woman is as obvious as the phone in front of your face. As a matter of fact, it is the phone. More specifically, it is one of the many optional features offered by the phone company. It's called *Call Forwarding*. This feature makes it possible to transfer calls from the users home address to any desired location. This is a method of trickery practiced almost exclusively by the cheating man who lives alone. One of those men is Michael. He is a cocky 26–year–old who has more women then he can handle. "I love the idea of living alone and being able to give my number out to several women," he boasts. "The only problem is they always seem to call at the worst time." What he's complaining about is frequency and inappropriate timing of his phone ringing. These random disturbances have caused him many close calls in the past. But now he has the solution, the old "Call Forwarding" technique. Too bad he didn't have it installed two months ago. It could have saved him a lot of embarrassment and humiliation.

> It was 7:00 pm on a Saturday night and I was preparing to have another victim, I mean, a nice young lady over for dinner. Since it was our first date I decided to impress her with my specialty, baked pork chops and steamed vegetables. I even bought a fresh loaf of Wonder bread to mark the occasion. After setting the table and filling the ice trays, I decided it would be a good idea to double check to make sure my girlfriend hadn't left any items over from the night before. You know, the usual womanly items—jewelry under the pillow, panties rolled up in the sheets, and curling iron under the bathroom sink. By 7:30 the coast was clear. I sprayed a light mist of Glade air freshener, poured myself a drink, and waited for Janet to arrive.
>
> At eight o'clock sharp, the doorbell rang, it was Janet. And she looked good enough to eat. Her hair was freshly cut and the mini dress she had on left nothing to the imagination. It was tightly fitted with a split on the side. Any mortal man would have attacked her right then and there, but not me. I'm very patient about coming on to a woman. The fact is, when you're sleeping with two and three women at a time, it's a luxury you can afford. Anyway, we sat down in the living room and got acquainted for a few minutes before having dinner.

It was the usual small talk about work, hobbies, and current events. All the while I'm staring at her, wondering what she would look like naked and on her back.

By 9:00 we had finished eating the extravagant dinner I had prepared and were back in the living room listening to the radio and talking. I offered her a drink of Tanqueray and grapefruit juice to loosen things up a bit, which she accepted. After a few sips, I started to get frisky and decided the time was right to make my move. That's when the phone rang. I excused myself and nervously went to answer it, hoping it wasn't this woman named Kim who I had faked out twice that week.

"Hello," I whispered.

"Hello Mike, this is Ben."

"What's up Ben, thank God it's you."

"What are you talking about?"

"Remember that young lady I told you about last week?"

"Yeah, what about her?"

"Well, she's here. And I'm trying my best to get into those pants."

"In that case, take care of business. I'll talk to you later. Don't forget to tag it a couple of times for me."

Immediately after hanging up, I turned off the phone and switched on the answering machine, which was in the hallway. When I walked back into the living room Janet's glass was empty. Of course, I suggested a refill, which again she accepted. But this time I made it much stronger, hoping to get her a little tipsy. Before long, things began to warm up. I had my hand high on her thigh and she was playing touchy feely with the hair on my chest. Just as I was about to move in for the kill the answering machine started clicking and beeping like crazy.

The last thing I wanted to do was put her on the defensive. And jumping up and down to make all of these adjustments was doing just that. I excused myself once again and dashed into the hallway to unplug the answering machine. My only option was to put it in the bedroom where she wouldn't hear it. Now, before you ask why I didn't simply turn it off, let me explain something. I am the assistant manager of a large retail store and one of my responsibilities is making out the work schedule. If one of the employees decides they can't make it to work, for whatever reason, I need to be aware of it as soon as possible to cover their shift. Not to mention the fact that turning off my machine would only arouse the suspicion of my other lady friends who know I always keep my machine on.

After setting up the answering machine on the nightstand next to my bed, I splashed on some Obsession cologne, closed the door behind me, and took a deep breath, hoping Janet wouldn't be ready to go. To my surprise, she was sitting comfortably on the sofa sipping on her drink. I apologized for the interruption and refreshed my drink before joining her. Within five minutes we were all over each other, pawing and grunting like wild animals. The sexual attraction was there and we both knew it. I picked her up caveman style, and carried her into the bedroom, better known as "The Bone Room." I quickly got undressed, put on my protection, and for the next 30 minutes we "knocked boots" like two newly released state prisoners. "Heaven must be like this," I thought as our bodies collided. However, my heaven was about to turn into a living hell. While we were taking a short break from the action, the phone rang, and the answering machine picked up. (Click, click)

"Awe Hell!" I thought. "The machine is in here with me. Please God, let that be Ben or my mother calling." Needless to say, it wasn't. And to top it off, I had accidentally turned up the volume. The following message was loudly broadcasted throughout my bedroom.

"Hello Michael, this is Kim, remember me?" an angry voice sarcastically inquired. "I'm the woman who you stood up tonight? Pick up the phone if you're there. What's wrong, are you too busy screwing some stupid slut you just met? If you are, I sincerely hope it was worth calling off our date. Anyway, make sure you call me in the morning when you get in, or should I say, when you get out?"

How embarrassing! Janet sprang up out of the bed in one motion, put on her clothes, and stormed out of my apartment. That was the last I ever saw or heard from her. I wonder why? I called the phone company the very next day to order call forwarding, and I have used it ever since. Now, whenever I have company I simply forward my calls to my pager. And when I'm expecting an important call, I transfer them to a friends or relatives house. I made a promise to myself never to get busted like that again.

The cheating man has a terrible habit of allowing his smaller head to do all the thinking. His uncontrollable passion has blinded him to the fact that his failure at cheating has little to do with complex methods. It is intelligence he is lacking. However, these crude tricks of the trade are very effective on those women who are simply passing through. Which is exactly how most men perceive them anyway. As brief sexual pit stops on the way to the ultimate piece. James, who is an executive for a pharmaceutical company, has been making pit stops all over the world for the last ten years, trying to find the perfect fit. At 39 years of age, he has slept with more women than he can count, but says he still isn't satisfied.

He bragged openly about his extraordinary ability to use various tricks to keep the women in his life in check. "A tool is only as good as the Mechanic," he boasts. "If you give an idiot a million dollar wrench, it won't make a damn bit of difference if he doesn't know which screw to turn." (Remind me to use that one). As a man who travels extensively, James often has female guests in from out of town who sometimes stay over night at his home. And up until recently, he had a good rotation with no problem or headaches. But that was before Sheila arrived on the scene. She disrupted his entire program and thoroughly convinced him that call forwarding was an absolute necessity. After all the hell she raised, he should have nicknamed her Oh Sheila!

> It was late Friday night when I arrived home from Toronto. My head was spinning and my feet were killing me. Four cities in five days, what a trip! After putting away my clothes and luggage, I walked over to my answering machine to check the messages. One by one I listened to eight boring messages from friends, family, and women I didn't give a damn about. Finally, I got the one I had been hoping for.
>
> "Hello James, this is Sheila, remember me? We met at the airport. I was calling to inform you I would be back in town again next Monday. Maybe we can get together for drinks or dinner after work. I'll give you a call when I get settled in my hotel room, bye."
>
> "She actually called!" I said while shaking my head in total disbelief. I would've bet a million bucks she was married, or at least seriously involved. She was about

six feet tall, with a slender build, and the most beautiful light brown eyes you would ever want to see. What a knock out! I damn near missed my flight trying to get acquainted. "Oh well, at least she took the initiative," I thought. It was up to me to take it from there. And I did just that.

When Monday rolled around, I found myself overly anxious to hear from her again. Although I didn't have to go into the office that morning, I woke up at 6:30 anyway to hit the gym for a good workout. I wanted to be very impressive on my first date with Sheila. After 30 minutes in the weight room, 20 minutes on the treadmill, and 15 laps in the pool, I felt like Hercules. I quickly toweled off, took a shower, and rushed home, hoping not to miss her call. Just as I walked through the door, the phone rang.

"Hello James?" she said as if to inquire.

"Yes this is James."

"Well, hello handsome, this is Sheila. How are you doing?"

"I'm fine," I cordially responded. "Have you checked into your hotel yet?"

"No, I'm still at the airport," she said in a frustrated tone. "The limo is late as usual."

"I'm off today, would you like for me to come pick you up?"

"No, don't bother. I'm sure my ride will be here shortly. But I'll tell you what, how about having dinner on me after work this evening?"

"Sounds great!" I said. "But only if you promise to allow me to pick out the wine."

"You've got a deal," she laughed.

We decided to meet downtown at 6:30 pm at one of

my favorite restaurants. They serve the best blackened catfish in the city and the atmosphere is very elegant. After saying our goodbyes, I went to work picking out my sharpest suit and tie. I even went to the barber shop for a fresh hair cut. It's not very often you meet a woman who makes you feel like a teenager again. By 5:30 I was pressed to a tee and the Mercedes was waxed up and ready to go. As I drove down the highway listening to my favorite oldies station I seriously asked myself, "Is it possible that such a beautiful and attractive woman is still on the market?" What I would soon discover was that she was entirely too available.

When I arrived at the restaurant, Sheila was sitting near the indoor pond reading a magazine. There was absolutely no mistaking who she was. Every man in the room, whether he was black, white, Hispanic, Asian, or Indian, was looking in her direction contemplating making a move, but it was too late. I casually walked over to where she was sitting and cleared my throat to get her attention.

"Excuse me, I'm James."

"Oh, I know who you are," she seductively replied. "I saw you out the corner of my eye when you walked through the door. It's nice to see you again."

"Likewise," I said, trying not to seem overly impressed.

"Well, shall we eat?" she said while reaching out for my arm.

"You took the words right out of my mouth. I'm starved."

It was apparent from the look on both our faces that the satisfaction was mutual. She was even more stunning than I recalled. And of course, I was looking dapper. To make a long story short, dinner was great and the conversation was even better. She told me she lived in New York, and that her company has an office here in New Orleans. She also made it clear there was no one special in her life. When she said that, I could practically feel the horns protruding out of the top of my head. I was the man for the job, and I was going to make damn sure she knew it. After drinking every drop of the dinner wine, and exchanging suggestive stares, I invited her out to my place for a night cap. One thing led to another and by the time the night was over she was looking up and I was looking down, if you know what I mean. The way I understood this relationship was this, we would have sex whenever she was in town on business, period. Which, according to her was only once a month. In my mind this was not going to constitute a serious commitment. Remember, I said in my *mind*.

Two months into this distant love affair, one thing became painfully obvious, Sheila wanted a more serious relationship. Those once a month business trips quickly turned into twice a month, and then every week. My bachelor lifestyle was being sabotaged. And to make matters even worse, she insisted on staying out at my place instead of downtown at her company's expense. In the beginning it didn't present a problem, since she arrived in town on Monday morning and was usually gone by Wednesday afternoon. But once again, her schedule was drastically changed to make my life miserable. Weekday stopovers suddenly became weekend vacations. And her temporary space in the closet began to resemble a secondary wardrobe. Any blind man could see I was headed for big trouble.

After two months of these regular weekend visits,

my social life began to go downhill. One of my lady friends left me for another lover, and I began to notice a dramatic decrease in the number of incoming calls. At first, I didn't think much of it, figuring I was just going through a dry spell. That happens every six months or so. However, this dry spell was turning into a drought, and there was only one person who could be held responsible, Sheila. She was taking up entirely too much of my time. I couldn't even answer the phone between 7:00 pm Friday and 5:00 pm Sunday. Hell, I began to feel like a married man. But what really made me uncomfortable was leaving her in my apartment unsupervised for an entire afternoon. During the month of August I was scheduled to be a guest speaker at various seminars and workshops. As it turned out, this was all the time Sheila would require to ransack my apartment and undermine my affairs.

It was the last weekend in August when everything came to a head. Sheila was visiting as usual and I had a 12:00 noon appointment across town. Once again she was going to be left *Home Alone*. However, this episode turned out to be more intense than the movie. On this particular Saturday morning, I was running very late and forgot to clip on my pager. "No problem," I thought. "I can simply retrieve my messages off my answering machine." At 3:00 pm I took a break from the meetings and phoned home to check my calls. But instead of the machine picking up, Sheila answered. Needless to say, I was pissed.

"Sheila, what in the hell are you doing answering my phone?" I angrily asked. "I specifically told you to allow the machine to record the messages, didn't I?"

The phone went silent for a few seconds. Then she

went into her act of trying to explain herself. Unconvincingly, I might add.

"The only reason I picked up the phone in the first place was because I was, uh, expecting a business associate to call me back. We have an important meeting on Monday morning and I wanted to, uh, go over a few notes with him."

"That's nothing but a bunch of bullshit," I thought. She could have just as easily given him her cellular phone number. It wasn't as if she couldn't afford it. Something fishy was going on, and I knew just how to catch her in the act.

"Look baby," I said, sounding as if I was buying her story. "After you receive your important call, I want you to turn the machine back on and allow it to answer the phone, ok?"

"Ok sweetheart. I'll be sure to do that. By the way, what time should I be expecting you?"

"Things are running way behind schedule down here," I lied. "I may not make it home until 7:00 or 8:00."

"That's too bad honey," she said sounding pleased. I wanted to get an early start on dinner. Oh well, I guess I'll see you around 8:00 then, bye."

It was obvious she was rushing me off the phone. Women are forever snooping around a man's apartment looking for whatever they can find to connect him with another woman, or they're just being nosy in general.

Immediately after hanging up the phone, I apologized to the chairman of the organization and rushed home. As I approached my home, I decided to park the car around back so Sheila wouldn't see it. I quietly came in through the back entrance and into the laundry room. And there she was sitting in the middle of the couch with my photo albums on one side and my phone book on the other, just as I expected. Meanwhile she was yapping it up on the phone with one of my lady friends as if they were bosom buddies. I stood there and listened as she lied about our relationship.

"Yeah girl, I don't know why James didn't tell you about our engagement. Personally, I think he's just a little jittery about settling down. You know how men are. No he's not in right now, but I'll be sure to tell him that you called. By the way, what did you say your name was again, Sara?" Well Sara, I'm glad we had this opportunity to talk. There's no sense of you wasting anymore of your valuable time calling on James, he's already taken."

That was all I could take. I stormed into the room, snatched the phone out of her hand, and told her to pack her bags. She tried to apologize, but I wasn't hearing it. When the taxi arrived, I courteously opened the door and kicked her crazy ass out. The very next day, I contacted the phone company and had Call Forwarding installed. Better late then never, I always say.

Keeping in touch with the other woman is no simple task. It is often an extremely irritating and stressful process which submits the cheating man to a perpetual life of intimate warfare. With the introduction and eventual copulation of each new lover comes a renewed battle with the suspicious wife or girlfriend to see to it that his whorish plans are not interfered with. Pagers on, phones off, answering machines turned down, and calls transferred. Whew! It's enough to make your head spin. But that's just the tip of the iceberg. Once he has resolved his communication problems, the desperate and horny cheater must face yet another difficult assignment, devising a plot that will justify his leaving out of the house long enough to "Get Busy." That's the whole point, isn't it?

THE ESCAPE

Many women may view "The Escape" as an overly exaggerated term to describe the man's desire to get away to see the other woman. However, if you present this same expression to the man who cheats, he will understand precisely why it is ideal. Past experiences have taught him that getting away to fool around is not so easy, especially if he's married or shacking. Carefully thought out excuses must be devised to explain his temporary or overnight absence. However, formulating these elaborate alibis can get downright stressful for the cheating man who often begins to see his home as a prison. A prison constructed in his own mind with the bars of his deceitful lies and the cement of his uncontrollable passion.

As the night's secret rendezvous draws nearer, the walls seemingly begin to close in. His comfortably furnished living room is subconsciously transformed into a cramped jail cell. "What in the world can I tell her to get out of here tonight?" he contemplates. As the clock ticks, the tension mounts. The man of the house now sees himself as the inmate of the house, likewise the innocent wife or girlfriend is also transformed. Where there once stood a docile woman in hair rollers, now stands the fierce warden with the keys to his freedom. What drama! And to think, all of this hallucinating over the fact that he wasn't allowed to "Go out to play." Well, since the warden, I mean, the wife or girlfriend will not issue a temporary pardon, the distraught cheating man must devise his own plan of escape.

Sporting events such as baseball, basketball, and football are the most common excuses used by men to lie their way out the house. Supposedly, they are either watching or playing. My guess would be playing. And since one or more of these sports are being played year round, they have become the perfect alibis for getting out both day or night, winter or summer. Hell, some men will even throw in a little lie about watching Golf or WWF if it will serve their purpose. Reginald, who is 27 years old and married, is one of these men who loves to play. Like so many of his cheating friends, he has discovered that sporting events provide the absolute best excuse to get out of the house and into the bed of the other woman. Here is an example of how he uses the method of escape men refer to as, "Playing Ball."

> When I want to use a sporting event as an excuse to get out, I arrange to have someone call my house about an hour or so before game time. For example, if the game comes on at 7:00, the call comes in at around 5:30 or 6:00, get the picture. The time factor is very critical since receiving phone calls too early or too late would make leaving out of the house even more awkward. Another important part of the set up is choosing the right caller. I prefer someone who my wife is familiar with, like a close friend or co-worker. Having a perfect stranger call is a definite no no. The last time I used this scheme was last weekend. I planned a hot date with my lady friend Karen at 7:00 p.m. Friday. She was bragging all day about turning me out so you know I had to get away to shut her up. At 6:00, my best friend Brian called. I made sure my wife was in position to answer the phone. This way she could identify who it was. After they said their hellos, I went into my act.
>
> "Brian, what's up? A basketball game you say? Who's playing? The Bulls and Knicks huh, cool! It won't be the same without watching Jordan slam dunk on Starks, but I'm all for it."
>
> I made sure to talk as loud as possible so that she would overhear our conversation. I didn't want her to get the impression it was my idea to go out. When she

tried to walk out of the room, I followed her around the house with the cordless phone. This performance was especially for her and she was going to hear all of it whether she liked it or not.

"So, what time did you say the game starts, seven? OK, I'll bring the chips and pretzels, you supply the beer. I should be there around 6:30, see you later."

Talk about academy award for best actor. There I was running off at the mouth about our fake plans while Brian was holding the phone laughing his ass off. Once the presentation was complete, I casually began putting on my blue sweat suit, which just happened to already be ironed. Meanwhile my wife is giving me one of those suspicious looks. But because I've done such a great job of acting, I fool myself into believing I'm actually going to watch basketball. Is this intense, or what? As I walked towards the door, I put on my Bulls baseball cap to look authentic.

"See you later baby," I said. "Don't wait up!"

"Ok sweetheart," she said sarcastically, "have a nice time with *the boys*."

"Now, what the hell did she mean by that remark?" I thought as the door shut behind me. At the time, I didn't give a damn. I was a free man, and Karen was anxiously waiting with nothing on but the radio. I got in my car, put in one of my old Isley Brothers cassette tapes, and hit the road. At 7:00 p.m. I arrived at Karen's apartment just in time for the tip off. As usual she had the television tuned into the game but my mind was elsewhere. I wanted to commit a few flagrant fouls of my own, if you catch my drift. By halftime, I was boning her like a real Gamma Man. She was screaming so loud the neighbors must have thought someone was trying to kill her. Or maybe they figured she was an over zealous Bulls fan. Who cared? At 10:30 I washed up, put on my clothes, and headed home. "What a game," I joked to myself. But on this night, my wife would take me into overtime.

OT

When I walked in the door she was still awake watching television. My first impulse was to run to the bathroom and check myself out, but I wanted to act normal. So I calmly hung my jacket in the closet and went over to give her a kiss. But before I could put my arms around her, she began questioning me about the outcome of the game.

"So, how was the game?" she asked.

"It was great! The Bulls looked pretty good tonight.".

"Yeah, they did alright," she said. "But they need a stronger bench."

"Since when did you start watching basketball?"

"I watch it all the time," she said sounding smart. "But I guess you wouldn't know that since you're gone every time there's a game on. By the way, did you see that vicious dunk Scottie Pippen made in the second quarter?"

"Oh shit!" I thought to myself. I was so busy laying the pipe to Karen that I forgot to take in a few of the highlights of the game. She had me with my pants down, and I sensed that she knew it. But instead of accusing me of outright lying, she played it cool and allowed me to cut my own throat.

"No, I must have missed that when I made a run to the store for more beer."

"What about that clutch free throw Horace Grant

missed in the fourth quarter? I couldn't believe he missed it."

"I couldn't believe it either, baby. You would think a professional basketball player could at least make a lousy free throw."

"Oh, and what about that hard foul Charles Oakley gave B.J. Armstrong at the end of the game?"

"Yeah, that was pretty bad. I don't know why the Knicks play so physical. It's like watching football."

Why in the world did I say that? I fell right into her trap. She grabbed the remote and switched the television channel to ESPN sports station. Right on cue, the basketball highlights came on. She gave me a nasty stare and excused herself to go to the bathroom. I stood there like a fool while the sports announcer commented on the Bulls game. "What was the big deal?" you ask. Well, the Bulls played alright, but against the Charlotte Hornets. Needless to say, I flunked her unexpected pop quiz. That incident taught me one very valuable lesson. "Don't forget to watch a little ball while you're out Playing Ball."

There are some men who have a very serious problem trying to keep their lies straight when it comes to Escaping, especially the novice cheater. His methods and techniques are crude and simple-minded. One of his most brilliant tricks is to have someone call pretending to be from his job. That may work, but what if the wife or girlfriend has a calculator and is keeping track of his extra work hours? Moving right along, his next attempt is to use the stupid excuse of, "I'm going around the corner to buy a lottery ticket." This won't do him much good unless his mistress lives downstairs or across the street, which some do. Otherwise he will not have adequate time to perform his manly duties. However, if he is bold enough to stay away for two hours using this weak alibi, he damn sure better return home with the winning ticket in his hand.

Finally, there is the inconsiderate and tactless approach to Escaping. In this situation the macho cheating man will simply head for the door proclaiming, "I'm going out, I'll be back later." I would advise any man who is dumb enough to constantly use this method to take certain precautions. First, walk out of the door backwards to avoid being hit by flying objects such as frying pans, knives, and of course the ever popular high heeled shoe. Secondly, buy a new set of clothes because yours will be out on the front lawn when you return. And lastly, figure out a secret entrance to get inside your home after the locks have been changed. It won't be long before any woman will snap after being treated so disrespectfully. Now that we have exposed the men who have no business playing the cheating game, let us turn our attention to those who have advanced degrees in infidelity.

The expert cheater sees the obstacles of Escaping merely as challenges to be overcome. Instead of complaining to his friends about how difficult it is to get away, he utilizes his ingenuity and imagination to develop a well laid out plan to set himself free. After careful consideration, he decides only one method of Escape will do, "The After Work Getaway." This technique is most commonly used by the cheating man who is either married or shacking. The way it works is simple. He calls home to tell his usual lie about working overtime and then leaves directly from work to see the other woman. And sometimes he'll simply tell his wife or girlfriend ahead of time that he has plans. After all, he doesn't have to disclose the specific details of those plans, right?

The reason why this particular method is so popular, is because the man is able to avoid the intense drama of explaining why he has to leave out of the house again. No man wants to be subjected to the guilt feelings of getting dressed to go out in the presence of his woman, especially since he's not taking her with him. The mere site of him standing in the mirror, combing his hair, and splashing on his most expensive cologne will surely piss her off. Meanwhile a subtle inspection is taking place to check that his attire is appropriate for hanging out with the boys, and not for picking up skeezers. She will definitely know something is up if he changes out of his stained boxer shorts into the silk bikini briefs he's been hiding in the bottom of his drawer. Of course, this entire situation can easily be avoided if the proper arrangements are made ahead of time.

One of the most ingenious methods men use to avoid going home to change is taking an extra set of clothes to work, better known as "The hide the clothes in the trunk trick." There isn't a cheating man alive who hasn't tried this trick, at least once. The problem, however, is sneaking the clothes inside the car without getting busted. One man said he waits until his wife falls asleep. Another man was so desperate he folded his garment bag up and placed it inside the garbage. Now that's ridiculous. But even after the clothes have been successfully smuggled out of the house, there still remains yet another problem. That's right, wrinkles. I don't care how neatly you hang them up or lay them down, those annoying creases always seem to find a way into your clothes.

But wrinkles are the least of the cheating man's worries. He is more concerned with finding a place to change into Super Man without alerting his co-workers to his secret plans. He doesn't want folks in his business, and you know how nosy they can be. Therefore, he is often limited to less than adequate accommodations to put on his expensive suit and silk tie. And you would not believe where some of these places are. McDonald's restaurant bathrooms, filthy gas station restrooms, cramped back seat of cars, and yes, even dirty alley ways. There is no extent to which the cheating man will not go to play the role of a single man. Which is exactly why he cannot go over to his mistress' house to change. He has boasted about having an understanding at home and does not want to appear to be sneaking out. "To hell with that," I say. "It's better to swallow your pride than to get dressed in a disgusting restroom or alley."

The single cheating man who lives alone is no less pathetic. He too must devise clever methods of Escape to keep his playboy facade intact. Lawrence, who is 34 years old, is the perfect example. He began dating a very beautiful young lady four months ago and promised not to have sex with any one else. As a matter of fact, he also promised not to have other female guests over to his apartment. How stupid can you get? During the first two months of their relationship, he was loyal to his word. But after three months of this torturous treatment, he began to question his decision to be faithful. "Should I get rid of her all together?" "Or should I try to have my cake and eat it too?" Being the stud that he is, you know which one he chose. Could he continue to pull off this stunt without alerting his girlfriend to the fact that he is a no good, low down, dirty dog? Let's find out. The preferred method of cheating in this situation is a technique called "Nobody's Home."

> You would think that having your own place would allow for some sense of independence, but no. The second you lay down with a woman she starts trying to move in and stake a claim. I've been on my own since I was 21 years old. And I'm not about to give up my freedom just because some woman believes her multiple orgasms grant her the mineral rights to my penis. I don't really like playing these games, but women don't give you any alternative. They come on strong, get you all

worked up, and then drop a bomb on you. For example, I met this attractive 24–year–old woman named Terry about four months ago at the club. When the party was over, she came by my place at two o'clock in the morning and got in bed with me. After twenty minutes of kissing and grinding, I reached for my condom to finish the job. That's when she grabbed my hand and said, "I can't have sex with you unless we have a commitment."

What in the hell did she expect me to say at this point? I mean really, there I was lying in bed with a firm breast in one hand and a dick as hard as Chinese calculus in the other. I was liable to say anything, which I did. I promised her a monogamous relationship. And up until three weeks ago, I kept that promise. But everything began to change as she became more suspicious and possessive. She quickly developed the bad habit of trying to keep track of my every whereabouts, or as my nephew would say, she was clocking me. I couldn't even take a piss without my pager going off or the phone ringing. "Where have you been?" "Where are you going?" "What time will you be back?" Her insecurity was enough to drive a man to drinking, or as in my case, game playing.

And it only got worse as the weeks passed. Terry began showing up at my job without calling me. Then she called my house at 12:00 midnight every night for two weeks. Finally, she made the ultimate mistake of coming over to my apartment unannounced. At the time, I wasn't up to anything, but that was beside the point. She had to be put in check.

"I pay the cost to be the boss in this house," I said. "And I don't appreciate you dropping by without calling first."

"Baby, I was just in the neighborhood and thought I would surprise you."

"First of all, I don't like surprises. And secondly, you live and work more than 25 miles away from here. How in the hell did you just happen to be in the neighborhood?"

"Well, I was uh."

"Yeah, I didn't think you had an answer for that one."

That incident really made me upset. I should have dropped her ass right then and there but the pussy was too good. There had to be a another way.

Three months into the relationship I became desperate. So, I developed a strategy to have my cake and eat it too. One of my most effective moves was to volunteer for the rotating shift at work. This made it impossible for Terry to keep up with my hours and days off. When she called on Sunday afternoon, I told her I was on my way out the door. When she called on Saturday night at 11:30, I told her I was just getting in. After a couple of weeks of this alternating schedule, I felt comfortable enough to make a test run of the single life. My first guinea pig was Linda. She was a fitness freak I met at the health club two months ago. We had been teasing one another about getting together for months and the time was finally right. I invited her over for dinner on a Saturday night. Of course, she accepted.

First, I set things up by telling Terry I had to work that evening. Another precaution I took was to park my car three blocks away in another apartment complex. This may sound extreme, but Terry had a terrible habit of circling my neighborhood like a vulture. As I said before, she would see my car downstairs and show up at my door unexpected and uninvited. "Not tonight!" I vowed. The next order of business was to dim the lights and close the curtains. Even though I live on the 15th floor, I wasn't taking any chances. Terry was the type who would carry a pair of binoculars inside her glove compartment. I simply played it off by lighting candles appearing to be romantic.

At 8:00 p.m. sharp, just as I finished putting all my safeguards in place, the doorbell rang. I apprehensively walked to the door and looked out the peep hole, it was Linda. I invited her in, took her coat, and escorted her into the living room to have a seat. She was dressed very elegantly. A long sheer dress, high heels, and nice accessories. I pay a lot of attention to details. After she was situated, I offered her a glass of wine, which she promptly accepted. It was a relief to finally meet a woman from the gym who wasn't one of those health nuts afraid of getting a little bubbly every once and a while. "So far, so good," I thought. Not long after we finished our first drink we began to click. She was open about her passion for contemporary jazz, hard exercise, and wild sex. "What a coincidence," I laughed, "those are my favorite hobbies too." I decided to impress her with my CD collection, so I played the latest from Sting. While she got into the music, I refreshed our drinks and casually unbuttoned my shirt so that she could get a good look at my chest.

By 10:00 we had finished eating and were relaxing on the living room floor. She asked for something to get comfortable in, so I gave her one of my T-shirts. Luckily for me, my longest one barely covered her ass. Up to that point, things were going smoothly with no interruption, until about an hour later when the phone rang. The answering machine picked up, but there was no message.

I didn't think much of it, and went back to sweet talking Linda. About thirty minutes later, while we were in the living room listening to Ronnie Jordan, there was a gentle knock at the door. "Oh Shit," I thought. I was thankful that we were quietly talking with the stereo playing low. I excused myself and walked towards the front. When I got to the hallway, I quietly tiptoed up to the door and looked out the peep hole. Can you believe I found Terry with her ear pressed up against the door? That blew my mind. She must have waited for someone to open the outer door, or either pushed a bunch of buttons until someone buzzed her in. You know how easy that is. Judging by the look on her face, she wasn't able to make out any sound, but she knocked again anyway. I took a deep breath and walked back into the living room trying not to look distressed.

"So who was at the door?" Linda asked.

"It's just one of my obnoxious neighbors," I lied. "He always drops by to borrow things and talk my ear off."

"How long is he going to keep knocking?"

"He'll get the message in a minute or two," I prayed. "Don't mind him."

I guess she bought it, because she didn't ask any more questions. And besides, Terry quit knocking shortly thereafter. As the night went on, her clothes came off. I felt like a free man again, if only for one night. She turned out to be everything I expected, mentally and sexually. I was sure this wouldn't be the last time we saw one another. "All I have to do is keep the lies flowing smoothly," I kept thinking to myself. "And I can have it all." When the time had finally come to say good night, I reluctantly walked her downstairs to the front entrance. I kept worrying that Terry was going to jump out from behind a door or something. After she made it safely to her car, I breathed a sigh of relief. "I made it through my first trial date without being busted," or so I thought.

The following morning was bright and sunny, perfect weather for car washing. When I walked outside, I was momentarily stunned because my Jeep wasn't out front where it is usually parked. Then I remembered that I had to hide it from Mrs. Ear to the Door. As I approached the far end of the lot, I could see it right were I left it, parked between the large dumpster and U-haul moving van. "I was really trying to bury that rascal," I laughed to myself. After checking to make sure all the tires were still on, I got inside and started up the engine. That's when I noticed the note under the windshield wiper. It read as follows:

"You picked one hell of a place to park. What's the matter, are you driving a stolen car or something? By the way, I came up to your job to surprise you with dinner, but I can see you decided to *eat out* instead. I hope you can survive off hamburger from now on because as of today you're all out of steak."

Needless to say, I was totally shocked. My first reaction was to jump out the car and double check for damage. I also looked under the hood for a bomb, just in case. After making sure everything was ok, I got back inside, shook my head and declared, "I'm getting too old for this shit!"

This life of the single cheating man is indeed an intriguing one. He is a sexual villain who insists on entertaining at home where he can impress the women with his cheap art work and King sized brass bed. His refrigerator is thoroughly stocked with all kinds of alcoholic beverages to help loosen up the sexual inhibitions of his victims. Yes, he's made absolutely sure his little sex trap is nice and comfortable. So comfortable in fact, his guest don't seem to ever want to leave. However, once playtime is over, he immediately begins plotting his strategy for her subtle evacuation. More to the point, he got what he wanted, now it's time for her to get the hell out.

Darryl is a 31-year-old police officer who has tried every trick in the book to get women out of his home. One of his favorites is to have a fellow officer call from the station to leave an official sounding message on his answering machine concerning extra duty assignments. Then he plays it back as loud as possible so the woman will hear it and get the idea to leave. On a few occasions he has gone so far as to put on his entire uniform and drive around the block until his guest was out of sight. Come on men, is it really that serious? Darryl says it most definitely is. In his words, "Women don't have the courtesy to leave when their welcome is worn out. Sometimes they need a little encouragement." Which brings us to the final trick of Escape. It's known as "Don't you get the hint?"

> Some men are too afraid to say what's really on their minds when it comes to Escaping, but not me. After the last orgasm of the night, mine of course, I begin plotting a way to skillfully ask the woman to get out. I call it "Putting her out with the cat." This may sound cold-blooded and ruthless to many women, but I don't care. It is the truth, whether they want to face it or not. Like most men, when I meet a beautiful woman I see her as the most desirable creature on earth. But as soon as I shoot my last shot, she is instantaneously transformed into a major nuisance, a pain in the butt. I don't give a damn how fine she is.

Last month, for example, I met this extremely attractive woman at the grocery store, of all places. Two weeks later we were in my bed sweating and grunting like wild animals. After the sex was over, she insisted on cuddling up and getting all mushy—I hate that. Then she started going on about how special she thought I was, and how she was looking forward to seeing me again. Meanwhile, I'm thinking to myself, "I wish I could blink like Bewitched and make this woman disappear." I know this may sound cruel, but I'm going to be up front about the way I feel. I have dealt with such a large number of women throughout my life, that I have adopted an assembly line mentality. Basically, I just want to process the woman from the door to the bedroom. Everything in between her arrival and the time we have sex is simply valuable time wasted. It's the same old routine. First I welcome her in and offer to take her coat. Then I ask her if she wants anything to drink. Of course, I will suggest something alcoholic to loosen up those already weak moral fibers. Inevitably the date will end with a long night of meaningless sex. But after the thrill is gone, I want her gone, it's that simple.

The worst part about this time consuming process is that frequently I am totally disappointed with the end results. Here I am wasting my valuable time trying to maneuver the woman into bed, only to find out she was barely worth the trouble. It's just like Eddie Murphy said in his stand-up comedy "Raw." He did an excellent job of describing how women try to trap men by holding out on the sex. Over a length of time, the man starts believing the woman's pussy is something special. "At first you think it's a Ritz," he joked. "But after you've eaten it for awhile, you find out that it's a plain old cracker." Once I find out that all I've got is a plain old cracker, my mind starts reeling with all kinds of schemes as to how I will get rid of the woman. Sometimes I'll yawn very noticeably to give her the hint that I'm tired. However, this doesn't usually work because most women see this as an invitation to offer to lay down with you. "Baby let's take a nap together," she'll say. It's times like that when I wish I could tell her I'm cramping and need to be alone.

I've also tried acting busy around the house hoping she would get the hint. But no! What does the woman do but ask if she can help out. Boy, that really pisses me off. I end up trying to dust and vacuum around her while saying, "Excuse me" every five seconds. And even if I do allow her to help, she doesn't know where anything belongs. She puts the forks where the spoons are supposed to be, and the Grits in the Oatmeal section. That just drives me all the more crazy. When all else fails, I resort to extreme tactics to escape this situation. One time I even went so far as to turn off the heat. She didn't last long with that thin sheet I gave her to keep warm with. Within 20 minutes she was making excuses to leave herself. Another time I had to practically starve the woman out of my house. The worst mistake I ever made was feeding her on the first date. Let this be a warning to men everywhere, don't ever let a woman find out you know how to cook. She'll be at your house so often you'll have to list her on your taxes as a dependent. And chances are she'll come over empty handed and hungry each and every time.

Trying to understand the way I feel is pointless for any woman. Only another man who has been where I'm at can relate. They know as I do, that it's not about being

> cold-hearted and insensitive. It's about having your space. Believe it or not I'd like to put aside these games long enough to really get to know someone, but right now I just can't. Even when I have genuinely tried to approach a woman with good intentions, I experience those same old feelings of frustration and annoyance. For example, the woman I mentioned earlier was attractive, intelligent, and generous. And to be honest with you, a damn good prospect for marriage. But two weeks into the relationship, I found myself wishing she would get the hell out of my bed so I could stretch out the way I really want to. All too often, the highlight of our date was hearing the door close behind her as she was leaving.

The idea that men actually have these cynical feelings will surely cause many women to shake their heads in total disgust and disbelief. At this very moment, you're probably asking yourselves, "Do men spend every waking moment plotting ways to fool around?" "Can it be that men are really this cold-hearted and calculating?" And more importantly, "Where do I fit into these schemes of Escaping?" Wait, before you try answering these and other questions, there is one last "Trick Of The Trade" or "Tale From The Dark Side," whichever you prefer. For his final feat, the cheating man of steel will leap over his wife or girlfriend in a single bound. In other words, "He'll try to sneak back into the house, take off his clothes, and slide quietly between the sheets without being detected. Sounds easy, right? I don't think so. It's not a simple matter of walking through the front door and announcing, "Honey I'm Home."

NIGHTCOURT

As the cheating man returns home from his night of mischief, he is consciously aware of the inevitable trial which will ensue the moment he sets foot through the front door. The wife or girlfriend, who should be asleep, will undoubtedly be waiting with a gavel and magnifying glass in hand. His humble abode will subsequently be transformed into Perry Mason's courtroom, and the case of the cheating man will be in session. In this court of law, the defendant is guilty until proven innocent, and the prosecutor serves as both Judge and Jury. Is this a no win situation or what? The trial begins with a subtle inspection for any apparent physical evidence of his unfaithfulness. Lipstick on the collar, the smell of a woman's perfume, and the dead giveaway guilt ridden look on his face. If she is unable to prove that he has been up to wrong doing based on these obvious signs, she will then build her case on circumstantial evidence. His coming in late from work, hurrying to get to the bathroom, and most incriminating of them all, his inability to "Get it up."

Of course, the cheating man is not going to take this sitting down. He will emphatically proclaim his innocence, "I plead not guilty!" Now it really starts to get ugly. The prosecuting wife or girlfriend begins aggressively cross examining the defendant, "Where were you? What were you doing? Who were you with?" These are clever tactics women use to see if the man will mix up his lies, but it won't work. He will either give her the old silent treatment, or submit an air tight alibi. "I went out to shoot pool with my friend Allen," he testifies. "We arrived at the pool hall at about 9:00 p.m., and left around midnight. Would you like to call him and verify my story?" Yeah right, like his buddy is going to tell her something different. He is a well coached cooperating witness for the defense. And besides, it's probably his night to act as the excuse man.

Once she is out of ammunition, or is simply too tired to go on any longer, there will be a continuance set for the following morning. In the mind of the guilty man, this is nothing more than a stay of execution. He knows it will only be a matter of time before the Hanging Judge convicts him of cheating in the first degree. Once convicted, he will likely receive one or more of the following sentences: House arrest, solitary confinement, or cruel and unusual punishment. In cheating man terminology this translates into: Not being allowed to go out for one month, sleeping on the sofa for two weeks, and being cut off sexually for an unspecified period of time. In that case, why not just give the poor guy a lethal injection or the electric chair and get it over with?

How far will a man go to hide the physical evidence of his crime? And how far will the woman go to uncover the truth? Well, based on what I have witnessed, there is absolutely no extent to which these two parties will not go to accomplish their goals. The cheating man, while guilty as hell, will do his best to cover any and all tracks of his unfaithfulness. The suspicious wife or girlfriend, who is not as stupid as the cheating man thinks, will prepare a case that would rival even the best L.A. Law episode. Who will win? Or are there ever really any winners? I'll let you be the judge of that. In the following case, Andre' is the defendant. He is 27 years old and has been married for three years. His wife, who has suspected him of cheating for the last six months, is the prosecuting attorney. On this particular night he would find out that tricks are for kids. All rise, court is now in session!

Debra, The Innocent Housewife
Plaintiff

-vs-

Andre, The Cheating Husband
Defendant

THE CASE OF
"The Truth Coming Out In The Wash"

There was one incident in particular when I felt that I truly did need a lawyer. It all began at 9:00 p.m. on a warm summer's night in August when I went over to my mistress' apartment for our usual Friday night sex date. As usual I fell asleep after she did one of her Jane Fonda aerobic numbers on me. When I woke up it was 2:00 in the morning. I quickly put my clothes on and shot out the door. By the time I made it home, it was 2:30. The smell of sex was all over me, and my hair was looking crazy. Right away, I knew what I had to do. The bathroom in the basement was my only chance of washing up without being busted. So, I walked around to the back door, and quietly slipped my key into the lock. As I pushed open the door, it began to squeak like hell. And the slower I tried to push it open, the louder it squeaked. Why is that?

Once I finally managed to get inside and make it downstairs, I quickly stuffed my clothes into the bottom of the hamper and jumped in the shower. For the next 20 minutes I thoroughly washed myself from head to toe. I had to make certain the sex smell was completely gone. After toweling off and finding a clean pair of underwear in the laundry room, I heard my wife Debra rattling pots and pans around in the kitchen. She was up for her late night inspection, but once again it was too late. All of the evidence had already been washed down the drain. I threw on my robe and confidently headed upstairs for a snack. When I got to the refrigerator, guess who was looking over my shoulder? No, not my wife, but Angela Lansbury of Murder She Wrote.

"Where have you been all night?" she asked.

"I was out, what's with the interrogation?"

"You said you were going to be out with David, but he called here at 10:00 p.m. looking for you!"

"We did plan to get together," I said confidently. "But I wasn't able to catch up with him."

"You two should do a better job of getting your lies straight."

At that moment, I couldn't have agreed with her more. I told his dumb ass I had a date that night and needed him to cover for me. I had to come up with a diversion, and fast.

"Wait one damn minute!" I demanded. "What about this filthy kitchen?"

"What are you talking about?" she said with a stunned look on her face.

"It's your week to wipe down the counters and wax the floor. But judging by all the crumbs lying around here, I can see you haven't done shit all day."

"What in the hell does that have to do with you coming in late?"

To be perfectly honest with you I really didn't know. My intention was to divert the issue, I was reaching for whatever I could find. And believe it or not, it worked. Before you know it, we were arguing over who washed the dishes and emptied the garbage last. By 3:30 I was exhausted. My head was spinning and my eyelids were getting heavy.

"This is pointless," I said while yawning. "You can stay up and argue by yourself. I'm going to bed."

She stayed downstairs pouting for another 30 minutes or so, then came to bed. No doubt frustrated by the fact that she couldn't break me down.

When I woke up the next morning, she was already downstairs doing laundry. I decided to vacuum the living room carpet and clean the kitchen. Ordinarily this was a foolproof way of getting back on her good side, but not this time. As I began running the water for the dishes, I heard Debra shout from downstairs, "I'll be damned!" About ten minutes later, she called for me to come down. As I approached the basement stairs, it dawned on me that I had forgotten to take my clothes out of the bottom of the hamper. "Oh well, it's too late for that now," I thought. When I opened the door to the laundry room, she had all my clothes from the night before laid out neatly on the folding table.

First there was exhibit A, the lipstick stain on my collar. Exhibit B, the smell of woman's perfume all over my sweater. Now, I could have probably come up with a quick and believable lie to explain those two items, but when she pointed out exhibits C and D, the phone numbers and condoms from out of my pants pocket, all I could do was throw myself on the mercy of the court. She was upset for weeks, but we managed to work things out. But why does it seem that no matter how hard you try to remember all of the tricks, one or two items always seem to find a way to slip by? Oh well, I'll have to be much more careful, **next time**.

Not every cheating man is fortunate enough to get away with sneaking in through back doors and jumping into basement showers. On the contrary, most men have to prepare themselves for an immediate inspection the second they hit the door. There is little or no time to suppress evidence. The wife or girlfriend, who is on constant alert, is waiting for the sound of his car to pull into the driveway to leap out of bed to deliver her opening statement. She has a bionic ear and can hear everything. A slow turning key in the door lock may as well be a noisy police siren. Alex, who is 27 years old, understands exactly what I'm talking about. He has been shacking for the past two years, and has a girlfriend who is prepared for battle at all times. She is a hair roller-wearing super sleuth with a keen eye for lipstick and foreign hairs. And because she is so preceptive, he was forced to raise his game to another level. As he put it, "If you've got a woman at home like mine, you better have your shit together when you walk in the door." I wonder what he meant by that.

Sonya, The Restless Girlfriend
Plaintiff

-vs-

Alex, The Composed Boyfriend
Defendant

THE CASE OF
"The Late Night Interrogation"

As I pulled into the driveway, I prayed Sonya would be asleep. But after taking a deep breath and slowly pushing open the door, I could see my prayer had gone unanswered. There she was at 1:00 in the morning with a pot of Folgers brewing on the stove and a empty box of No Doze on the counter. "Boy, I'm in for it tonight," I thought to myself. I played it cool and acted as if I had nothing to hide. Which of course, I did.

"Hi baby, what are you doing up so late?" I reluctantly asked.

"I heard a loud noise out back, and couldn't go back to sleep."

"Yeah Right," I thought. The only noise she heard was the sound of my car pulling into the driveway. I hung my jacket in the closet and headed for the stairs.

"Well, I'm going to take a shower and get ready for bed."

"Wait a second sweetheart, I haven't seen you all day. Can I at least get a quick hug?"

I knew what she was up to. This was her sly way of getting a sniff of my clothes and a close look at my collar. But of course, she was wasting her time. There was no evidence to be found.

When I made it into the bathroom, I turned on the shower and slowly began unbuttoning my shirt. And just as I was about to take off my pants, my wife abruptly walks in.

"Excuse me baby, I forgot to take my pill," she said while casually looking me over.

"Do what you have to do," I said trying not to laugh. I knew she kept her birth control pills inside her purse. This was just another one of her surprise inspections to uncover evidence. Maybe she was looking for lipstick on my underwear, who knows. Whatever the reason was for her unlawful entry, she came up empty handed once again. My body was odor free and my back was without scars.

After unnecessarily going through the medicine cabinet for five minutes, she suddenly remembered that her birth control pills were in the bedroom. "No kidding," I thought. But instead of leaving the room to give me some privacy, she stood there in the doorway observing my every move. I looked her straight in the eyes and busted out laughing.

"What are you giggling about?" she asked.

"Oh, nothing."

What I was laughing at was this detective role she was trying to play with me, and a bad one at that. I remember staring at her thinking to myself, "Ms. Sherlock Holmes really thinks she has her man tonight." But little did she know who she was dealing with.

You see, unlike most men, I don't worry about being inspected when I get home. I am extremely careful about concealing the evidence of my wrongdoings long before I ever set foot in the house. First of all, I don't allow women to lean on me if they have on heavy make-up or perfume. That means no slow dancing or close hugging. Secondly, my girlfriend buys the same brand of soap I use at home. Women know the difference between the smell of Coast and Caress, that's for sure. Anyway, back to Ms. Columbo. When I went back downstairs to grab a snack, she began questioning me about where I had been all night. Of course I had an air tight alibi. But then she threw me a curve by bringing up events from months long past.

"Remember when you came home back in April and I found that woman's business card in your pocket with her home phone number on the back?" she asked. "And what about three months ago when you told me you were going out with Derrick and he called here looking for you that same night?"

I was stunned. My confident grin turned into a look of complete confusion. All of a sudden the kitchen counter she was sitting behind started to resemble a Judge's Bench. I had to retaliate.

"What in the hell are you talking about!" I shouted.

"You know what I'm talking about!" You and Derrick are always up to something. I just haven't caught you yet."

"That is totally unfair Sonya, and you know it!"

Of course, what I really wanted to say was, "I Object!" But what was the point? She would overrule me anyway. I was clearly being railroaded with no jury of my peers to hear my case. The accusations and cross-examination continued.

"And what about that Saturday night back in June when you said you had to work? Not more than an hour after you left, your job called asking if you wanted to work overtime. Explain that one, Mr. Gigolo?"

Now I was really starting to get upset. Not because of her aggressive questioning, but because I knew I had perfectly good lies to explain those charges at the time. "Isn't there some kind of statute of limitations?" I angrily thought. I fired back fiercely, determined to turn the case in my favor.

"Ok, wait one damn minute!" I insisted. "You can't pull up all of these events from a hundred years ago just because you suspect me of cheating. Either you have proof or you don't. Otherwise, get off my back!"

Women know damn well a man can't keep up with his lies if they're more than a week or two old. This was simply her way of getting back at me for not being able to come up with concrete evidence. I had a solid defense and she couldn't stand it. After two hours of this non-stop Spanish Inquisition, she finally retired to her chambers, I mean the bedroom. When I woke up the next morning the case had been dismissed. No doubt due to the lack of proof. She apologized for her paranoid behavior and we left it at that. Now, let this be a lesson to cheating men everywhere, "Stand firm on your lies, and don't crack under pressure."

Hiding evidence from an intelligent and suspicious woman is no easy task. It is often a very painstaking and tedious process which challenges the cheating man to stay sharp at all times. He is aware of how easy it can be to overlook even the most obvious signs of wrongdoing. The visible long black hair on a white shirt, the flagrant aroma of Estee' Lauder perfume on a sports jacket, and the lipstick stained cigarette butt in the car ashtray are amongst the most common oversights. Of course, these slip-ups are only problems for those men who are either married or shacking. The cheating man who lives alone has obstacles which are unique to his situation. And these obstacles must be overcome if he expects to maintain his privacy and hold on to his many women.

Sam, who is 34 years old and divorced, understands exactly how different the cheating game is as a single man. In his words, "Living alone may exempt you from on the spot inspections, but you can bet your girlfriend will be dusting for fingerprints the moment she walks through the door." Like most men who cheat, Sam has promised not to entertain other female guests at his apartment. As a result of making this ill-advised verbal contract, he has subjected himself to periodic inspections of his premises. However, what worries him most is not his girlfriend's snooping around, but the devious practice other women have of purposely leaving items in a man's apartment for another woman to find.

Shelly, The Nosy Girlfriend
Plaintiff

-vs-

Sam, The Concealing Boyfriend
Defendant

THE CASE OF "Guess Who's Coming To Dinner?"

When you have an apartment as large as mine, concealing evidence of fooling around is easier said than done. With two bedrooms, two baths, a large den, and a patio you can just imagine how easy it can be to overlook one or two small items. Like most bachelors who put a great deal of time and energy into decorating, I like to show off my entire place. So, I make sure to utilize each and every room when entertaining guests, if you know what I mean. Sometimes I start in the den, stroke it a few times in the bedroom, and then move the party outside onto the patio. It all depends on how freaky I feel. However, these sexual escapades almost got me in big trouble three months ago. Talk about close calls.

I had just come in from walking my girlfriend Shelly to her car when the phone rang. It was Rhonda. Her voice was deep and sexy, just as I remembered. It had been six months since we last talked or had wild sex. I figured she was calling for her 3,000 mile tune-up, and I was right.

"So, what's up for tonight?" she asked.

"I don't know baby, you tell me."

"Well, I just got back from vacationing in California,

and I was hoping we could get together. You know, like old times.

"Is this a booty call?"

"Let's just say it's a body call. My body's calling for you."

"In that case, stop stalling and bring that thing on over here."

"Cool!" she said sounding excited. "Do I have a time limit or is this going to be an over nighter?"

"You won't be in any condition to go home tonight, trust me."

"Don't let your mouth write checks that your dick can't cash."

"I think my record speaks for itself," I said confidently. "And by the way, if you want a cocktail bring it with you. All I have in the fridge is beer."

"Baby, all I need is a cold can of Sam," she said in a seductive tone. "A sixteen ounce, if you please."

"Ok, that's enough of this 1-900 phone sex," I said. "I'll see you at 10:00 p.m., bye."

Immediately after hanging up the phone, I transferred my calls to my pager and turned off the answering machine. I know all those little tricks of the trades, you know. At ten o'clock sharp, the doorbell rang. I looked through the peephole and there she was, standing with her hair pulled back into a ponytail, looking good enough to eat. When I opened the door, I could tell she was hot as hell. The mild aroma of her womanly juices filled the air, and she had that, "I'm going to fuck your brains out" look in her eyes. Before she could barely get out of her sweater we were all over each other. I damn near tore the button off my jeans trying to get undressed. We went from the dining room table to the kitchen counter, and then onto the living room sofa. I was determined to make her toes curl. This sex duel went on until 1:00 in the morning. I can't tell you who won, but we both came out on top.

First thing in the morning Rhonda jumped out of bed, drank a cup of coffee, and was off to pick up her daughter for church. I got up to lock the door behind her and went back to bed. Hell, I didn't have anywhere to go. At 11:30 a.m. I finally got up and cooked a late breakfast, my battery needed recharging. After eating a meal fit for a King, I turned on the tube and watched a couple of basketball games. They were playing a double header on NBC. But it wasn't until 5:00 p.m. that I realized my phone hadn't rung all day. I called my voice mail service and dialed in my code. The electronic voice said I had four messages. I sat back sipping on a cold beer while I listened.

(Beep) "Sam, this is Larry. I just called to let you know the game was on, talk to you later."

(Beep) "Wake up lazy, this is your mother. You have some mail over here, call me when you get up."

(Beep) "Hi baby, this is Rhonda. I had a great time last night. I hope I didn't break anything. Call me later on if you get a chance, bye."

OK, everything seemed to be under control. But there was still one last message to retrieve before I could go back to watching my game.

(Beep) "Sam, this is Shelly, I'm at the grocery store. I have one last stop to make before I get there. It's about 5:00 now, so I should be there about five thirty, quarter to six. Oh yeah, the store was all out of ranch dressing, so I picked up a small bottle of French, just for tonight. See you shortly, love you."

Needless to say, I was completely stunned. There I was kicking back as if I didn't have a care in the world and my woman was going to be walking in the door in less than an hour. Evidence was lying all over the place and the aroma of women's perfume was in the air. I quickly threw my beer in the garbage and snatched my cleaning rags from under the bathroom sink. "It's time for the white tornado," I humorously thought to myself. The joke, of course, is that I am black. Get it?

For the next few minutes, I was a blur moving swiftly from one room to the other. Beginning with the bedroom, I changed the linen, put away my condoms, and sprayed air freshener. "Scent of a woman" isn't just the name of a good movie, you know. Sometimes it can be the most incriminating evidence of all. Next, I replaced the towels in the bathroom, wiped all female type hairs out of the sink, and emptied the trash. Then, it was on to the kitchen to wash the lipstick off of the glassware and make sure that any signs of two people eating or drinking was covered up. Finally, I went back to the bedroom to check if Rhonda had left any items such as jewelry, clothing, or other personal belongings. And sure enough, I found her white Teddy hanging in the very back of the closet. As I stuffed it into the bottom of my sock drawer, I shook my head thinking "Women really think they're slick."

Since Shelly hadn't arrived yet, I decided to quickly vacuum the living room carpet to give it that overall clean and innocent look. In 35 minutes, my house was spotless. I tossed the dirty linen into the washer, put away all of my cleaning rags, rolled the vacuum cleaner into the closet, and sprayed half a can of lysol in the air. "Whew, I did it," I said proudly to myself. Just as I was about to jump into the shower, the doorbell rang. I ran out of the bathroom half naked, unlocked the door, and ran back. "Come on in," I shouted. I wasn't about to let her get a whiff of me before I had a chance to wash up. I knew she would be looking for any clues she could find. One time I even caught her going through my garbage. Talk about being nosy.

After reading these pitiful stories of how men cheat, many women out there will undoubtedly ask, "Why would any man go through so much trouble?" Well, some men see it simply as the price to be paid for cheating. They have become so accustomed to the process that it hardly phases them. "But why play these games at all?" you ask. The answer to that question would of course depend on which man you ask. Each man has his own individual reasons for cheating, there is no universal explanation. One hundred men would likely give you one hundred different excuses. However, there isn't enough room in this one book to investigate them all. So I investigated the four most common explanations men use for being unfaithful. This was not a simple task, let me tell you. With so many causes and effects, who could expect to cover them all? Nevertheless, I do believe I was successful at representing the attitudes of most of the cheating men who are still at large.

So, without any further ado, prepare yourself for what will surely be a conscious raising experience. One which will open your naive eyes and forever change the way you view infidelity. But be warned! There are both responsibility and expectations for those who insist on access to the naked truth. No longer will you be able to sit back and declare, "I didn't know." With the knowledge of how and why the game is played, you may be challenged to leave your cheating man altogether, or forever shut up and go along with the program. The choice will be up to you.

CHAPTER 2
CREATING A MONSTER

Like any other negative behavior, infidelity is learned from watching and imitating bad examples. Show me a cheating father and I can probably show you a cheating son. However, infidelity is not simply a reaction to negative influences, it is also a choice. A choice which has more to do with low morality than complex psychology. But regardless of what the reasons are for this deceitful conduct, one thing is absolutely certain, there is no such thing as a born cheater. The question then is, "How was he created?"

IT STARTS AT HOME

Any woman who is seriously interested in understanding why her man cheats, should begin by examining his upbringing. It is quite possible he was raised by parents who have accidentally or purposely planted negative impressions in his mind concerning the way in which women are to be treated. And with the help of ignorant relatives and narrow minded friends of the family, he could very well be ruined for life. The miseducation of the young male usually begins with the so-called "Men of the family." They are usually the first to offer their pessimistic views on today's woman. First there's good old uncle Charlie, "All women are good for is cooking, cleaning, and making babies. And don't ever trust them either. They're born liars, every one of them." Then cousin Jesse adds his two cents, "Women only want you for your money," he warns. "When it's gone, they're gone."

Of course, much of this worldly advice is based on nothing more than chauvinism and their own failed relationships.

Nevertheless, they pump the inexperienced young man full of this garbage and send him out into the world with a prejudice and disrespectful attitude towards women and relationships. And if that's not bad enough, the lovely ladies of the family also add to this brainwashing. They too have a terrible habit of talking negatively in the presence of the impressionable young man. Aunt Betty, who always has her nose in other peoples business, comments about the neighbors, "I can't believe that woman downstairs just had another baby. I'll bet a million dollars it's not her husband's." Cousin Barbara responds, "At least she's not screwing her boss trying to get a promotion like someone I know." Now, if this type of dialogue doesn't strengthen a young man's belief in the virtue of women, I don't know what will.

It's hard to believe that not long ago the family home was the primary school of respect and good manners. Treating young ladies with honor was a required course for graduation into manhood. But all that seems to have changed. Today's parents, much like our school systems, no longer appear interested in properly educating their young males. They set horrible examples and throw up their hands, surrendering them to the streets. As a result, boys are growing into men who are emotionally malnourished and morally bankrupt. How in the hell can we expect these miseducated and misguided souls to handle the day to day workings of an adult relationship? It's virtually impossible! The lazy and irresponsible parent then has the nerve to ask, "Where did I go wrong?" And more importantly, "Is there any chance my son can alter his behavior?" Not likely. Those who have witnessed years of negative examples aren't as easily deprogrammed as you may think. They are by-products of their families and environment and this is at the root of who and what they are. As the saying goes, "The fruit doesn't fall far from the tree."

Most men would prefer to leave their family history out of it when it comes to explaining why they cheat on women. No one wants to blame good old Mom and Dad for doing an ineffective job of raising the perfect gentleman. And besides, they know that using their background as an excuse for infidelity will not wash over well with the 90s woman, who is anxiously waiting to pick her teeth with the skeletal remains of his conniving carcass. Therefore, let me make it perfectly clear that neither of the men who I interviewed is expecting women to sympathize with their experience. The whole idea is to establish a starting point from which to begin examining why men are so unfaithful. As Dorothy from The Wizard Of Oz would say, "There's no place like home."

Raymond, who is 28 years old, comes from a long line of unfaithful men. His grandfather was a cheater, as was his father and uncles. And like so many other young men raised in this environment, he would inevitably become a cheater too. "After so many years watching the men in your family get away with it, you begin to perceive it as normal," he says. Well, normal or not, he has successfully fulfilled the family legacy of infidelity. And with two sons of his own, it would appear that there will be heirs to the cheating throne. The question is, when will it ever end?

> My father was a very intelligent and charismatic man who taught me everything I know about women. How to hold them, talk to them, and unintentionally, how to cheat on them. At the tender age of twelve, I began taking notes. First, there were the secret phone calls in the basement. My father always made sure he got as far away as possible from my mother's ultra-sensitive ears. The conversations were always brief and coded. He would say five or ten words and hang up. Within an hour after every call he was out the door.

When my mother asked him where he was going, his excuse was always the same, "I'm going to play cards." To make his alibi appear more authentic, one of his brothers would call to confirm that he was playing poker or bid whist. But he became annoyed with being questioned every week, so he decided to sneak out the back door and avoid being interrogated. It was funny watching a grown man tiptoeing out the house like a kid who was on punishment.

As the years passed, my father's unfaithfulness became more apparent. I found all kinds of evidence such as condoms, secret telephone books, and pictures of him with other women hidden behind old albums and underneath the bar. "Parents are so stupid," I thought. "Don't they know you can't hide anything from a kid." But his most daring feat of all was seducing the neighbor's wife. I believe it was the fall of '81 when Bridgette and Steve moved in next door. They were a real odd couple. She was 5′ 9″, full figured, with dark brown hair that came down to the middle of her back. Whereas he was short, slightly overweight, and going bald. My father wasted no time in trying to cozy up to Steve. Twice a week they watched football and drank beer together. He even helped paint his living room. However, this buddy buddy business was only a front. My father was using Steve to get next to Bridgette. I knew it was only a matter of time before he succeeded. And sure enough, his opportunity came when Steve went on the graveyard shift—12-8 a.m.

Within a week of this new schedule my father had him timed perfectly. At 11:30 Steve walked out of the front door, and at 11:31 you know who came in through the back. From my bedroom window, which looked out into their back yard, I watched the whole thing like a comedy sitcom. He would creep out of the back door like a cat burglar and into Bridgette's bedroom window. One time he was so horny, he jumped over the fence instead of walking around to the gate. While all of this excitement was going on, my mother never suspected a thing. She was accustomed to my father staying up late drinking beer and listening to music. And on the few occasions when she happened to wake up and catch him coming in, he would give her the old line about checking for prowlers. Of course, the only prowler who needed to be checked was him. This went on for six months before Steve became suspicious. And who do you think he came to for advice? That's right, my dad. I could have died laughing as I listened in from the kitchen while they talked outside on the deck.

"Gary, I just don't know what to do," he said sounding depressed. "I know something is going on but I can't put my finger on it."

"Are you sure it's not just your imagination, Steve?"

"I'm not sure about anything these days. This midnight schedule has me walking around like a damned zombie."

"If I were you, I'd stop worrying so much and try to get some rest. Bridgette loves you and would never do anything to jeopardize your marriage."

"I guess you're right."

"I know I'm right!" my father said convincingly. "You've got a good woman there, trust me."

"I'm glad we had a chance to talk, Gary. I was ready to pack up and take a job offer in Seattle."

"No, don't do that!" my father slipped. "I mean, why would you want to leave all your friends and family behind? This is your home."

What a masterful job he did of securing his next door piece. Steve seemed completely fooled by this speech about loyalty and trust. Nevertheless, my father backed off for a few weeks, just in case. What a smart decision this turned out to be. Steve took days off of work and doubled back several times trying to catch her in the act. But a few weeks later, when things finally cooled down, my father was leaping over the fence and into Bridgette's window once again. This affair went on for two years until Steve decided to take the job in Seattle. On a cool autumn Saturday afternoon he packed up his moving truck and drove off into the sunset with his furnishings and my father's mistress.

Those incidents all took place many years ago and today I have a family of my own. A beautiful wife and two handsome boys ages 6 and 4. When I decided to get married, I promised myself to be the perfect husband. No lies, no tricks, and no women on the side. However, old habits and family traditions die hard. Two years after saying "I do," I was out there doing the exact same things my father did to my mother. Whispering on the telephone, sneaking out of the house, and fooling around with married women. For years I didn't want to admit it, but I guess it's true. I'm a chip off the old block.

For an increasing number of young boys in our society there are no positive male role models at home to emulate. As a result, women have been left to the difficult task of trying to mold their sons into respectable men with little or no help. And try they do, often times with great results, thank God! However, it must be said that not all mothers have been so successful or even concerned about the proper upbringing of their son(s). In fact, many of them have only helped to create another generation of cheaters. "How is that?" you ask. By using the wrong language and living by a bad example. Remember the old saying, "Do as I say and not as I do?" Well, you can just forget about that nonsense. Young males aren't so easily conditioned. They see Mom as a sacred goddess who must be perfect in every way. That means no cursing, no drunkenness, no drugs, and definitely no promiscuous sex. Failure to live up to this flawless image of motherhood may cause the son to become bitterly disappointed and resentful. He will conveniently use every harsh word and immoral act as an excuse to justify his own unethical conduct. And when the guilty parent tries to confront him with his wrongdoing, he will wisely redirect the issue, "How come it's ok for you to do it, but I can't?" The mother's response is always the same, "Because I'm grown, that's why." In the analytical mind of the young boy this answer is weak and unacceptable. He believes that adults, especially his mother, should act more responsibly and lead by example, not words.

As the young man enters into his adolescent years, the need for a positive parental image is particularly important. This is the period when the impressionable teenybopper is struggling with his own sexuality. "Is sex a game, a weapon, or a mutually shared act of love?" he ponders. His answer will depend a great deal on how his mother conducts her intimate affairs. If he lives in a household where men are disrespected and sexually manipulated, his inclination may be to treat women in the same manner. Cedric, who is 29 years old, grew up in such an environment. Throughout his childhood he listened and watched as his mother used and abused men without an ounce of shame. These corrupt sights and sounds contributed significantly to his cheating mentality. And like most men who have bad memories of their mother's behavior, he remembers every detail as if it were yesterday.

Watching my parents split up as a 10-year-old was bad enough without the added burden of dealing with all the bitter feelings floating around. The divorce was supposedly mutually agreed upon but you never would have known it by the way my mother verbally attacked my father. She talked to him on the phone like a dog, calling him all kinds of MF's and SOB's. I hated the way she treated him, and I told her so on numerous occasions. Shortly after the divorce was final, my mother's lifestyle began to change. She started smoking, drinking, and hanging out with a new set of friends. They were loud and obnoxious women who pried into our family business every chance they got. Her two nosiest girlfriends were Bertha and Agnis, names which fit them perfectly.

Bertha was 5'3" and weighed about two hundred pounds. She had a terrible habit of taking off her shoes when she came to visit. Her feet smelled like a combination of spoiled government cheese and hot garbage. The only good thing about the aroma was that it killed the cockroaches and ran away the mice. Agnis was even worse. She had very bad skin, bad breath, and yellow teeth. When she tried to give me a kiss, I would run out the back door. But their appearance had nothing to do with why I despise them. It was their constant degrading of my father, whom I loved very much. Their conversations about him were mean and unwarranted. The one I remember most took place a week after the divorce. Fat ass Bertha instigated the whole thing.

"So Valerie, how much alimony and child support did you get from that cheap bastard?"

"Not as much as I asked for," my mother responded.

"You can take him back to court for more money if he gets a raise. You know that, don't you?"

"Don't worry, he's not getting away with one thin dime if I can help it."

"What about visitation?" Agnis asked.

"Well, the judge said every other weekend, and two months during the summer. But I'll decide when and if he can see Cedric."

"I like your attitude girl," Bertha said. "He doesn't deserve to see his son after the way he treated you."

That statement upset me for two reasons. One, she didn't know my family well enough to make that judgment. And two, my father treated my mother like a queen. She was the one neglecting her responsibilities at home and running the streets. Besides, I was taught that family business should stay within the family. She was violating her own rules. Subjects which had never been discussed with outsiders was now being openly broadcast without consideration for who heard it. My perception of women was never the same after that.

Two years and a thousand bitter conversations later, my mother finally met someone who could put up with her hostile anti-male attitude. I'll call him John. He was a very nice man who was never too busy to talk or toss a baseball around. But what I liked about him most was that he never once said anything derogatory about my father. My mother acted completely different around him. Dressing up in sexy outfits, talking very politely, and cooking meals like Betty Crocker. "She never went through all of this trouble for my father," I thought. "Maybe they would still be together." Oh well, as long as she was happy, I was happy. And besides, with John in her life I expected some of the pressure and hostility to be directed away from my father. Unfortunately, this was not to be.

My mother took every opportunity to rub my father's face in her new love affair. Sometimes she would intentionally call him by John's name. And on a number of occasions, she made plans for the three of us to go out of town during the weekends of my father's visitation. John never knew about this scheme, otherwise I'm sure he would have put an end to it. These acts of mental cruelty went on for about six months until, guess what? That's right, my mother came up pregnant. Things were about to get interesting, very interesting! John wanted to get married, but my mother was dead set against it. The decision was made to keep the babies and address the issue of marriage at a later date. Oh yeah, I did say babies. My mother delivered twins, two girls. For the next few months life seemed perfect. Mom was excited about being pregnant, John was as proud as can be, and my father and I were spending more time together. However, it wasn't long before this blissful life came to an abrupt end.

A year or so after the girls were born, my mother broke up with John. She said he was smothering her, but I knew this was only an excuse to get rid of him. Her mood turned gloomy, and her patience thinned. The whole situation exploded. My father was back in the dog house and now John was right there with him. This was the point in my life where I specifically recall thinking of my mother as a bitch. Not in a disrespectful way, mind you, but she was giving these guys hell. And low and behold, guess who reappeared again, those nosy instigating wenches. "Do these damn women only materialize when my mother is depressed?" I wondered. "I guess it's true what they say, misery loves company." Boy, was I ever getting a lesson in commitment 101.

Here you have two decent men, seemingly trying to do the right thing, and the woman is dogging them out. This was a complete reversal of what people typically see going on in relationships. But as time went on, things got even worse.

By the time I turned sixteen, my mother had become a ruthless gold digger. She was determined to get what she wanted no matter how many men she had to go through. When the basement needed remodeling, she dated a carpenter. When her car broke down and needed major repairs, the carpenter was dumped for a mechanic. And when she wanted to spend the rent money to get her hair and nails done, she dated the landlord. Meanwhile, I'm sitting back watching everything. The lies over the phone, the late night rendezvous, and the promiscuous behavior. She may not have been sexually involved with all of them, but she was definitely giving it up to somebody. Witnessing all these lies and games caused me to lose what little respect I had for my mother. Deep down inside, I thought of her as an irresponsible parent and materialistic whore. And on several occasions she only helped to reinforce my perception.

The day of my 18th birthday was the most dramatic of all the negative sights I had seen of my mother's loose behavior. I chose to spend the night at my father's house for the weekend to celebrate. We went bowling, to the movies, and out to dinner. My mother wasn't expecting me back until Monday morning. But because of a power outage on Sunday night, our visit was cut short. I tried calling home to let my mother know I was on my way home, but there was no answer. When I arrived home at 7:30 p.m. I understood why no one could hear the phone ringing, there was a wild party going on. The music was loud and strange people were all over the place drinking and smoking marijuana. The only familiar face in the room was big Bertha. I tapped her on the shoulder to get her attention. Needless to say, she was surprised to see me.

"What are you doing here!"

"What do you mean, what I'm I doing here? I live here, goddamit. Where is my mother and the twins?"

"Your sisters are with the next door neighbor."

"And what about my mother?"

"I think she's upstairs, I'll go get her."

"I don't need you to play messenger," I said with an attitude. "This is my house."

"Wait Cedric, don't go up there."

When I made it to the top of the stairs, I could hear voices coming from my mother's bedroom. When I knocked on the door, a strange man's voice forcefully asked, "Who is it?" That's when I put my broad shoulder to the door and pushed it open. What I saw was disgraceful. There, lying on the bed buck naked, was my mother. She had a joint in one hand and the man's penis in the other. And no, this man was neither the carpenter, the plumber, or even the landlord. That I could have dealt with, maybe. But this was a guy I had never laid eyes on. My first reaction was to swing the door back shut. I just stood there in shock while my mother excused herself to put something on.

"I'll be right back," she told him.

"Who in the hell was that anyway?" he asked.

"My son."

"Your son! You didn't tell me you had a son."

"She's got two daughters too!" I yelled from the hallway. "I guess she didn't tell you that either."

My mother came storming out of the bedroom and dragged me to my bedroom. But instead of explaining to me in a calm manner about what I had just happened, she had the nerve to ball me out as if I had done something wrong.

"Who do you think you are by busting into my bedroom like some kind of mad man?"

"How was I supposed to know you would be in there fucking somebody?" I angrily replied.

Smack! She slapped me across the face and grabbed me by the shirt.

"I'm the adult in this damn house, you understand. "I pay the rent, I buy the food, and I put the clothes on your back. So don't you get smart with me!"

I was so pissed, I couldn't even bring myself to cry. I wanted badly to pop her upside the head, but that was still mom. So, I got myself under control and calmly began packing up my belongings. Things were getting too deep for me around there, and it was time to leave. Meanwhile, my mother was standing with her hands on her hips, as if she thought I was bluffing. Within fifteen minutes I had stuffed as much as possible into my bags. I pulled the car keys out of my pocket and headed for the door. Everyone in the party stopped what they were doing to watch the show.

"Where in the hell do you think you're going?" my mother yelled.

"To my father's house!" I shouted. "I'm eighteen years old and I can live wherever I choose."

"You're not taking my car."

"Here," I said as I flung the keys violently in her direction. "I'll walk if I have to."

"Calm down, Cedric," Bertha said as she put her hand on my shoulder.

"Get your hands off me bitch, you don't even know me."

I gave my mother a mean look, grabbed my bags, and walked out the door. When I made it to the corner gas station I called my father. He must have run every traffic light because he made a half hour drive in less than twenty minutes. On the way back to his house, my mind flashed back to all the terrible things my mother had done throughout the years. First, I thought about how disrespectfully she treated my father. Then I remembered the cold-blooded way she dogged poor John. Finally, there were the disturbing memories of all the men she used and had been used by. I promised myself that day, never to allow a woman to get close enough to break my heart or take advantage of me the way she did so many men throughout her life. And to this day, I haven't.

The negative influences of what goes on inside the family is often compounded by what goes on outside. This area is more contemporarily known as "The Hood." This is the space through which the gullible young boy must travel to get to and from school, the candy store, and the concrete basketball courts. Here is where the hardcore lessons of life are administered. How to walk with an attitude, cock a baseball hat to the side, and how to perceive young girls as bitches and hos. These destructive and disrespectful classes are taught on the streets each and every day. And while the irresponsible adults are off somewhere drinking, partying, or screwing, the Hood gradually becomes the most powerful force in molding the young man's mind. Many desperate parents have packed up and moved to the suburbs hoping to shield their sons from these negative influences. However, their efforts are often in vain because bad examples exist everywhere. The Cassanova business man who lives next door is just as negative a role model as the womanizing pimp on the city street corner. Remember, all images are potentially dangerous when left unchecked.

Television, better known as the idiot box, is also a contributing factor in male infidelity. This electronic entertainer, educator, baby sitter, and brainwasher has a great deal of influence on our everyday lives. It tells us what to buy, where to pay it, and who's got the best price. But what it also does is alter behavior. Consider this, young males between the ages of 13-18 watch an average of 36 hours of television a week, that's a little more than 5 hours per day. During this time they are bombarded with images of extreme violence, abusive language, and blatant acts of promiscuity. And with the addition of cable, they have access to literally hundreds of degrading programming 24 hours a day. When I was a kid growing up in the 70s, we were lucky to get 7 channels. And that was only if you had a good VHF and UHF antenna. The examples of promiscuity were limited to the secret agents and street pimp characters. James Bond, In Like Flint, The Mack, and Superfly were among the most popular. But today, it is the Rap and Rock stars who have been promoted to the status of surrogate parents and role models.

Ask any young man what BET or MTV is and he can tell you. These are just two of the ever-increasing music video channels which broadcast hours of artistic and not so artistic images. Young boys are drawn to these sights and sounds like hormonal magnets. With all of the butt slapping, titty grabbing, and dissing of women going on, who's surprised? Even many adult men are glued to the television like zombies. And while some critics may argue that art simply imitates life, I say it also has the ability to define it. Now, I don't mean to sound like some old fart who opposes the freedom of Rap and Rock artists to express themselves, but let's get real. Some of that stuff is downright disgraceful, don't even try justifying it! The bottom line is this, parents must stand up and take responsibility for properly raising their sons. Otherwise the television, and the streets, will do it for them.

I would be remiss if I concluded this chapter without exposing the adult cheating man who also receives support for his scandalous behavior at home. Despite the fact that his relatives know full well that he's married or shacking, they allow him to frequently invite his whores and mistresses over to their homes to engage in sex. The men of the family, who are often cheaters themselves, sympathize with the horny relative and provide him with a warm bed and clean linen to do his dirty deed. As one 40–year–old uncle said, "We men must come together in our time of need." I guess he was referring to sexual needs. But what about the righteous women of the family? Would they condone such disrespectful conduct? You're damn right they would! As a matter of fact, more men admitted to having used their mother's, sister's, and aunt's home for sex than any other relatives. This is just another example of women working against one another. While wives and girlfriends all over the world are complaining about the no good cheating man, these shameless female relatives are conspiring with their brothers, sons, and nephews to work out weekly sex schedules to carry out their affairs. Close your mouths, you know who you are.

Some of you do it because you don't know how to tell him no. But often it's simply a case of, "Why not?" After all, you probably don't like the way his wife or girlfriend is treating him anyway. And hey, he might even return the favor someday, right? This type of mentality plays right into the hands of the cheating man who needs all of the support he can get to remain irresponsible. With an unsuspecting woman at home and a loving relative to "Watch his back," he can go on like this forever. The surroundings are comfortable, familiar, and most importantly, economical. One woman's reaction concerning this issue was understandably bitter, "If my brother wants to lay up all day screwing his whores, his cheap ass will have to pay for a motel room." Unfortunately, there are far too many relatives who don't share her moral attitude. They will continue to allow the cheating man to use their residence as a whore house as often as he wants. What they fail to realize, however, is that by supporting his weekly sex habit, they are preventing the over grown little boy from developing into a halfway decent man.

NO MORE MR. NICE GUY

"Where are all of the good men?" women cry. Or more to the point, "Where are all the men who don't play games?" The answer to that question is simple, you've already passed them by. And if you haven't, you probably will. According to the so called "Nice Guys" whom I've interviewed, "A woman wouldn't know a good man if he bit her on the ass." Now, before you denounce this statement as just another angry verbal reaction from a few frustrated, unattractive losers, take your own personal survey. Begin by asking your brothers, uncles, and male co-workers. See if they concur with this assessment of today's woman. (Pause) Are you surprised that 99% of them are in total agreement? Well you shouldn't be, and I'll tell you why. It is a commonly held belief in the male community, that women are not looking for good men but are searching after superficial images. And these images must take on very specific characteristics. They must look a certain way, talk a certain way, and most importantly, present a challenge. "And if that's what women want, then that's exactly what they'll get," says the bad guy, who is more than willing to conform to the woman's warped sense of reality long enough to get what he wants. He will put on just the right outfit, deliver his most provocative line, and present himself in such a way as to cause the woman to wonder, "What's up with him?" Now all of this may sound somewhat diabolical, but guess what? It works like a charm. As one gentleman put it, "They don't call it the Dating Game for nothing."

The nice guy, on the other hand, has no premeditated plans of playing games or using women. He is confident his pleasant personality and respectful mannerism will attract a woman who will appreciate him. "To hell with all the game playing," he says. "I want to do the right thing." Of course, this was his attitude before he got dumped for the ump-teenth time, was stood up twice in one week, and witnessed the bad guys having all of the success. Suddenly, he feels the need to re-evaluate his position. Late at night while lying in bed alone yet again, the nice guy begins to cross-examine himself. "Will I continue to allow myself to be victimized?" he contemplates. "Or should I stop playing the fool and learn how to play the game myself?" Which one do you think he'll choose?

What experiences could cause a man to permanently or even temporarily vacate his position of nice guy? And what would make him decide that honesty is a sign of weakness and a disadvantage? The answer to that question is very simple, it's all a matter of observation. Just as the nice guy has examined the cheating man's rate of success, the cheating man has likewise observed the nice guy's complete and total failure. One look has convinced him that he wants no further auditions for the "Dudley Do Right" role. Vincent, who is 26 years old says "Amen" to that. He is sick and tired of being dogged out by women who claim to want a good man. As he put it, "Women don't appreciate good men anymore. They lie to you and play games just to get into your pocket." This is the attitude he adopted six months ago while at the night club. What began as a evening of fun and relaxation, turned into a very enlightening experience he would never forget.

> It was 10:00 p.m. when I arrived at the club. My feet were killing me from standing all day at work, so I was hoping to find a seat. Luckily, there were still three unoccupied tables in the back, directly across from the ladies room. I rested my jacket on the back of the chair, flagged down the nearest waitress, and ordered a pitcher of beer and Buffalo wings. But if I had known about the show that was going to take place later that night, I

would have ordered a box of Raisinettes and popcorn instead. At 10:30 p.m. my best friend Nate shows up, late as usual. I could tell by the look on his face that he was pumped up and ready to party.

"What's up Vince! he shouted. "I hope you're ready to throw down tonight."

"Sit your wild ass down, Nate." I laughed. "Pour yourself a beer and chill out."

"Good idea partner," he said while lighting up a cigarette. "Let's work on getting a nice buzz until more victims arrive."

Nate was a real dog but he always had great success at pulling women. And he isn't exceptionally attractive either. As a matter of fact, I'm much better looking. He is 5' 8", a little on the chubby side, and wears glasses. I'm 6' 2", slim, with 20/20 vision. However, picking up women has little to do with looks and more to do with attitude. Nate demonstrated that to me on a number of occasions. I may have been handsome and gentlemanly, but he had the most important characteristic of all, charisma.

By 11:30 p.m., the club had really started to jump. Nate and I, now full of Coronas and Tequila, grabbed the closest women we could find and shot out onto the dance floor. My sore feet had been magically healed with a little help from the alcohol and deep bass in the music. The DJ was really mixing it up. First he played a little Snoop Doggy Dog, then came back with a nice House jam. My dance partner was deep into the music. She took off her jacket and tried to show me up by doing the Percolator, so I retaliated with a new dance called the Butterfly. Meanwhile, Nate and his partner were standing around like two geriatric patients, swinging their hands from side to side. I don't know what in the hell they were trying do. It looked like a bad imitation of an old dance called the Spank. After 45 minutes of bumping, jumping, and sweating, we took a break. I immediately rushed to the men's room to freshen up and Nate went back to check on our table. The club had begun to fill up and no seat was safe from hostile takeover.

After wiping off my face and spraying on a fresh coat of cologne, I headed for the bar. The bartender was a tall good looking woman with thick lips. When she asked me what I was having, I wanted to say, "How about those lips, *on the rocks*." But instead, I ordered a screwdriver and kept from having my face slapped. While I sat there sipping on my drink, I glanced around the bar searching for good prospects, that's when Sharon caught my eye. She was sitting on the far end of the bar with two other women, both of whom were exceptionally attractive. I must have stared at her for at least 20 minutes trying to work up the courage to introduce myself. Women have no idea how uncomfortable it is for a man to approach them, especially when they're in a group. It's like walking into a den of lions. After checking myself in the mirror for the one hundredth time, I took a deep breath and made my move.

"Hello, my name is Vince, would you like to dance?" Without saying a single word, she grabbed me by the hand and led me onto the floor.

"I guess that means yes," I said jokingly.

The dance floor was completely packed with people doing the Electric Slide. We shoved our way through and joined in. It wasn't long before people were stepping all over my sore feet and scuffing up my shoes. The only benefit was getting a full view of Sharon's anatomy. She was tall, with big brown eyes, and a body like a hooker. And the outfit she had on was smokin', a gold sequin mini dress with matching pumps. What a sight! I wanted to marry her right then and there.

After 20 minutes of this boring dance the DJ finally slowed things down. I expected Sharon to rush off, but she surprised me by putting her arms around my waist and leaning against my chest. For the next three slow songs she whispered the lyrics in my ear and grind the shit out of me. I tried to keep my dick from getting hard but it was a losing battle. Half way through the second song I had a serious boner. When the dance was over, I quickly shoved my hand inside my pocket and escorted her off the dance floor.

"Thank you very much for the dance," I said trying not to look too embarrassed.

"The pleasure was all mine," she said with a seductive smile.

"If you have a minute, I'd like to sit down and get better acquainted."

"Sure, but let me go finish my drink and talk with my girlfriends for a second. Where are you sitting?"

"Directly across from the ladies room," I said while pointing.

"Ok, I'll meet you over there in a little while."

"Wait a minute!" I said. "I didn't get your name."

"My name is Sharon, what's yours?"

"Vincent."

"Ok, Vincent, I'll see you later."

As she turned to walk away, I took another look at her body in that tight dress. Boy was she ever filling it out. Her ass was so round you could have sat a drink on it and maybe even an ashtray. I jacked up my slacks and walked towards my table feeling like Joe Stud.

Getting back to my seat was no easy task. Women were all over the place trying to get in and out of the restroom. Meanwhile, the men were standing around with empty glasses in their hands blocking the isles. They were too cheap to get a refill and too chicken to talk to the women who were walking right past them. After excusing myself a thousand times, I finally made it through. Not surprisingly, Nate was sitting right smack in the middle of two tables full of women. He looked like a kid in a candy store.

"Man, do you see all of these women," he whispered. "I've already got three phone numbers and the night is still young."

"Well congratulations, Mr. Playboy," I said trying to keep my voice down. "Now, if you don't mind I'm going to need your seat for a minute."

"So, you pulled one huh Vince? I knew it wouldn't be long before I rubbed off on ya."

"Just take your no dancin' ass out there on the floor and try not to make a fool of yourself."

"Happy hunting, partner."

He took one last sip of his drink, and made his way through the thick crowd. Now I was left alone with a group of loud and flashy women on both sides of my table. Wouldn't you know that out of all the appealing females in the club, I ended up sitting next to the most obnoxious. Sure, a couple of them were good looking, but as it turned out, not very classy. The Broadway musical "Women from hell" was about to begin. How could I have ever known I would be the guest of honor?

For the next 30 minutes I looked down at my watch a hundred times wondering what happened to Sharon. I didn't want to believe she faked me out, but my faith was weakening with the passing of every minute. After waiting restlessly for another 15 minutes, I resigned myself to the fact that she wasn't coming. My mood changed from exhilaration to aggravation. "How could she play me like this?" I angrily contemplated. "If she wasn't interested she should have said so." Nate always told me never to get my hopes up too high when dealing with women. "They'll burn you every time," he would say. As I sat there with my feelings hurt, I decided to do what most men do, get drunk. All I wanted was a stiff drink and to be left alone. But the women sitting next to me had other plans.

"So, are you waiting for your wife?" one woman inquired.

"No, I'm not married."

"You must be waiting on your girlfriend, then."

"Well, I'm not exactly dating anyone seriously right now."

Why in the world did I have to go and say that? They were all over me like white on rice after that comment.

"Hey girls, he's single!" she broadcasted to her mob.

"Well, are you available or what?" another woman asked.

"Yes and no," I replied.

"Which one is it, sweetheart?"

"What I want to know is, do he have a job?" her illiterate girlfriend interrupted.

This interrogation was getting to be a pain in the ass. Some men may find all this attention to be very flattering, but not me. I'm not attracted to overly aggressive women, at least not ignorant ones. I politely told them I was expecting a friend, hoping it would quiet them down. And for a while, it did. But this was merely the calm before the storm.

The women who were piling in and out of the ladies room only added to my frustration. They were talking loudly and using very harsh language. As I listened in on their conversation, my young mind was both disturbed and enlightened. And because they had such big mouths, it was easy to overhear each and every word.

"Did you see that cheap ass dress that bitch was wearing?" said one woman whom you never would have expected to speak in such a way.

"Yeah girl, and she still had the price tag on it," her girlfriend laughed. She'll be taking that bad boy back for a refund tomorrow."

Then I overheard another woman schooling her girlfriend on how to take advantage of men.

"Girl, you should have left your wallet in the car."

"And how was I supposed to pay for my drinks without any money?" the girlfriend asked.

"Simple, do what I do. Find a man with some money, show him a little cleavage, and stroke his ego. He'll be buying you drinks all night long."

"Hmm," I thought. "So that's the game huh?" I put that one in my mental rolodex. Finally, there was a group of intoxicated black and Hispanic women coming out of the ladies room screaming.

"Where are all the real men?"

"Yeah, where are all the **real** men?" the women at the table next to me joined in.

At first, I bit my tongue hoping the men standing nearby would put them in check, but they were a bunch of wimps. So, being the frustrated, angry, and drunk son of a bitch I was at the time, I took it upon myself to singlehandedly defend the male race.

"Where in the hell are the real women?" I shouted back.

"The real women are right here," said one of the black women who was to be the biggest instigator.

"Real women my ass! One of your girlfriends is sporting a cheap hair weave, the other one has on fake nails, and your nappy headed butt is wearing blue contact lenses. So don't come up in here yelling about needing a real man. You've got to be real to see real."

The area exploded with laughter. The men were giving high fives and co-signing. Even some of the women applauded me for telling it like it is. As for the rowdy bunch who started the whole mess, well they somehow managed to slither their way to the opposite side of the club. I guess I must have hit a nerve.

Feeling somewhat redeemed, I polished off my drink and grabbed my jacket ready to call it a night. And just as I was about to go after Nate, guess who I see making her way over to my table? That's right, Sharon. After getting past all the big behinds and jealous looks, she sat her glass on the table and began explaining why she hadn't come over sooner.

"I wanted to come over earlier, but it was so congested over here I didn't think there would be any place to sit."

In my mind, that was bullshit. I should have cursed her out right then and there, but I didn't. Believe it or not, I was still happy to see her.

"Well, now that you're finally here," I said, "let me get right down to the point. Do you have a man?"

"No, not at the moment."

"You've got to be kidding me. A beautiful woman

like yourself without a man."

"It's true. All the men I meet are either married, shacking, or dealing with too many women. I don't have time for that. But what about you Vince? I know the ladies are knocking down your door."

"My situation is much like yours. I keep running into women who are into playing games. They claim to want a good man but what they really want is someone who will dog them out. So, lately I've just been concentrating on my job and taking care of my daughter. By the way, do you have any children?"

"Ah, no," she hesitated. "But I spend a lot of time with my nieces."

"What about work? Do you like your job?"

"Yes, I love my job. I work for a ah, marketing firm downtown," she hesitated again. "We do product advertisement for Revlon and several other cosmetic companies."

I thought her answer was rather vague, but at the time I was more interested in those seven digits than her resumé. After talking for a few minutes about our hobbies and favorite night spots, she excused herself to go to the ladies room. I could understand why she had to go so badly, her breath smelled like a brewery.

While I waited for Sharon to return, I searched for a pen and piece of paper to write my phone number on. That's when I looked up and saw Nate making his way back over to the table. He was sarcastically applauding and sporting this silly looking grin on his face. "Now what?" I wondered.

"Congratulations Vince, I see you got with the biggest skeezzer in the club."

"Who are you talking about?"

"That slut Tina I saw you over here talking to."

"You must be mistaken, her name is Sharon."

"Is that what that bitch told you? Her name is Tina. And she's been passed around more than a jar of mustard at a picnic."

"Tina!"

"Yes, Tina, and I'll bet she lied about having a job at an advertising firm or something like that, didn't she?"

"How did you know?" I asked curiously.

"She always uses that tired line. I guess she's embarrassed to tell people she works as a sales associate in the cosmetic department at Walgreens."

"What about kids? She told me she didn't have any."

"Oh please, give me a break!" he laughed. "That ho has three ugly little heathens at home, and they all have different fathers."

"You've got to be kidding me," I argued.

"I'm telling you the truth Vince. I met her about three months ago at a club on the north side. She was bragging to a lady friend of mine about how easy it was to find a sucker to buy her drinks whenever she went out. I guess she chose you for tonight."

"But wait a minute. If she wanted to take advantage of me, why didn't she come over with me after we danced?"

"Because another sucker was buying her drinks already. As a matter of fact, he was buying drinks for her girlfriends too. I guess his money must have ran out."

"I'll be damned, no wonder she smells like a tavern."

"Where is she now?" he asked.

"In the ladies room."

"Ok, this is what I want you to do. Wait until she comes back and see if she asks you to buy her a drink.

If I'm right, she'll ask for something very expensive. I'll be standing over on the stairs where I can see you."

At first, I didn't want to go along with this game. But the more I thought about all the lies she told, the more appealing it became. So, I settled down and tried my best to look and act normal. Nate didn't help matters much when he suddenly turned as he was headed for the stairs and asked, "By the way, what was she drinking when she came over?"

I picked up the glass she had come over with and examined it.

"It's water."

He turned and continued on his way to the stairs barely able to keep from pissing on himself from laughter. All I could do was sit there like a fool and think about how polite I had been to her, only to find out that I was being set up for drinks and God knows what else.

When Sharon, I mean Tina, returned from the bathroom she was refreshed and wouldn't you know it, thirsty.

"I'm back," she announced. "Aren't you going to offer a lady a drink?"

"Lady my ass," I thought. Little did she know I was on to her game. I wanted to blow up, but instead I played along with her masquerade to see how far she would go. When I spotted the waitress, I flagged her down and allowed Tina to order.

"May I take your orders?" she politely asked.

"Yes," Tina replied. "I would like a double shot of Martell and a Champagne Split."

"And what about you sir?"

"I'll have a Rum and Coke. And you can cancel that first order. Give the lady here another of what she's already having. By the way *Tina*, that is water isn't it?"

The poised look on her face quickly changed to utter humiliation.

"What did you call me?"

"Tina," I replied. "Isn't that your real name, you trifling bitch."

Nate must have read my lips because when I looked over towards the stairs he was laughing his ass off. Even the waitress was cracking up. Tina jumped out of her seat, gave me a sly grin, and took off without saying a word. But what was there to say? She was busted. After that altercation, I grabbed my jacket, shook hands with Nate, and went home. What a night!

The lessons from that night will stay with me forever. I learned that not only do nice guys finish last, but they also spend more money. I also discovered that women are incredibly good impostors. They dress themselves up to look like queens but in reality they're nothing more than well dressed pick pockets. And while I realize that not all women are as conniving and ignorant as those women I encountered at the club that night, I am wise enough to know that many of them do exist, too many. Now I can set aside this nonsense about treating them all with dignity and respect. From now on my motto is, "Burn them before they burn you." This may sound cold and immature, but I didn't create this world we live in, I'm only trying to survive in it.

Many men can relate well to the painful and humiliating experiences associated with the club scene. It is an environment where perpetrating and game playing is the norm. The nice guy is out of place in this manipulative setting and would be better off pursuing a meaningful relationship elsewhere. "But where is elsewhere?" The nice guy has been burned no matter where he has looked. Some of them have been introduced by mutual friends, while others have even tried meeting women through church. But regardless of how or where they meet, the same scenario seems to replay itself over and over again. The woman meets the man and claims to be interested. She insists on going out on several dates to get better acquainted, at his expense of course. For the next two months he takes her out to dinner, buys her clothes, and helps her move five rooms of heavy furniture across town. And what does he get for his trouble? A well fed, well dressed, unappreciative woman living in a well furnished new apartment. When he suggests getting intimate, she drops the bomb on him, "I just want to be friends."

After enduring so many of these emasculating experiences, the nice guy begins to see the light. Although he has been raised in a home where women were put on a pedestal, he can no longer pardon these continuous assaults on his manhood and his wallet. At last, his innocent eyes have been opened to the cold world of the material girl. Now he must take a stand and look out for his own interest. Jason can relate well to the negative feelings men can develop towards women as a result of their game playing. He is 34 years old and has been trying desperately to keep a positive attitude towards women and relationships. But the endless games have finally taken their toll. After years of being used and abused, he fiercely proclaims, "Chivalry is dead! Long live the barbarian!" Was he simply looking for an excuse to play the field, or was he driven to it? You be the judge.

> Throughout my life, I have dealt with many scandalous women. Some of them were terrible liars. While

others were just plain old no good. But there was one woman who put all of them to shame, her name was Jennifer. We met two years ago at a card party. My friend Stan, who is forever trying to play match maker, went out of his way to introduce us. He said we would have a lot in common. And as it turned out, he was right. We both loved working out, watching basketball, and playing cards. But what made us most compatible was that neither of us had children. I wasn't interested in a ready made family, and she didn't want to play the step mother role. "If I'm going to have a house full of kids spending my money and driving me crazy, you better believe they're going to be mine," she said. I couldn't have agreed with her more. Anyway, after discussing everything from hobbies to gang violence, the topics became more personal.

"So Jason, are you seeing anyone special?" she asked.

"To be honest with you, the answer is no."

"Explain to me how someone as handsome and intelligent as yourself has managed to stay single?"

"Well, at the risk of sounding conceited, I can't find a woman who meets my requirements."

"And what might those requirements be?" she asked while smiling flirtatiously.

"She must be attractive, honest, and physically fit. But most importantly, she must have a passion for basketball."

"Boy, what a coincidence! That woman sounds exactly like me. But hold on just a minute, Stan told me you only date older women. I'm only 27 years old."

"Hey, there's an exception to every rule."

Jennifer was a gorgeous woman with a wonderful

sense of humor. Any man would have changed his criterion to get with her. She had beautiful dark brown skin, long jet black hair, and a body that was built to last. Even the loose fitting jeans she had on couldn't disguise her small waist and big thighs. She was everything a man could ever ask for in a woman, and then some. As the conversation continued, I set aside physical attraction and concentrated on commitment. My facial expression became more serious and so did the subject matter.

"Look Jennifer, before we go on joking around with one another, I'd like to tell you how I feel about relationships."

"Fire away."

"First of all, I'm a very busy man with many responsibilities. I don't have the time or patience for game playing. I need a woman who is interested in building something."

"Well, I'm ready for a one on one relationship myself," she replied. "But I'm having the same problem you are, finding someone who meets my requirements."

"Ok, I'll take the bait, what are your requirements?"

"I want a man who knows where he's going in life, keeps himself well groomed, and can hold on to a damned job for more than six months."

Although her remark was very funny, I understood exactly where she was coming from. We decided to put our conversation on hold for the time being and enjoy the rest of the evening playing cards and telling corny jokes. She treated me like I was her man by fixing my plate and feeding me at the table. I felt as if I had known her for years. Some women have a way of making you feel that way. When the party was over, I gave her a hug, a kiss on the cheek and my phone number. She promised to call within a couple of days to arrange a date.

While driving home, I thought about how nice it was to meet her. I was also hoping she would be just as wonderful the next time we got together. No, I wasn't being pessimistic. But those second encounters can get rather tricky. I call it "Second Date Syndrome." That's when you notice all the defects which were either hidden or overlooked the first time. Some of these defects include the woman's butt appearing flatter or her breasts seeming smaller than you recall. Then there's the facial flaws, or the "Ugly Face," as I call it. This is when the night time beauty queen turns into a day time tire biter. It's truly amazing what a good nights sleep and a little sun light can reveal. Lastly, you have the most unfortunate change of them all, the personality switch. There is nothing more disappointing than discovering that the woman you felt so comfortable with has suddenly lost her pleasant personality and sense of humor. Most men blame these optical illusions and character misjudgments on poor lighting or too much alcohol. I was hoping this would not be the case with Jennifer. Well, a man can dream, can't he?

It was late Sunday night and I hadn't heard from Jennifer. I figured two days was long enough to wait before calling someone, but she obviously felt differently. By the end of the week I began making excuses for her. "Maybe she lost the number," I thought. Or "Maybe she was in a car accident." After ten days of waiting, my compassion turned to aggravation. I began to think she had lied to me about not having a boyfriend, but Stan assured me she was single. That being the case, there was only one other possible explanation, she was playing the old "Telephone Hesitation Game." This is how it works. The woman either requests or accepts a man's phone number with the promise of calling soon to arrange a date. She then *intentionally* waits days, if not weeks, to use it. During this time, the number is taken through a process more complex than the U.S. mail.

It is sorted out along with all the other numbers she has collected over the weekend and put in a category. Usually this is done in the presence of her nosy girlfriends to add a little fun to the procedure. One by one each man is judged based on physical attractiveness, personality traits, estimated income, and penis size. After careful deliberation, a verdict is reached. If a man is labeled as too ugly, too boring, too cheap, or too light in the pants his number will simply be thrown into the trash. Most women participate in this cold-hearted practice to one degree or another. And Jennifer was proving to be a part of this infamous sorority. "But why me?" I wondered. "What could I have done to deserve elimination?" At that point, however, it didn't really matter. All I wanted was the courtesy of a phone call. Just one lousy call, that's all!

After twelve days of subjecting myself to this mental cruelty, I copped an attitude. "To hell with her," I declared. "It's her loss." I sat around that entire afternoon and convinced myself it was over. And just when my mind was finally made up, guess who decides to call? That's right, Ms. Telephone Delay herself. I was hoping she was calling from either a hospital emergency room or a remote village in Africa. No other excuse would be acceptable.

"Hi, Jason, this is Jennifer, how are you doing?"

"Fine, how about yourself?"

"I'm doing great! Sorry I didn't get an opportunity to get back to you sooner, I've been kinda busy."

"Well, I understand how it is. Everybody has their priorities," I said sarcastically.

Little did she realize that my fond attitude towards her had been drastically altered. She was all over me at the party like a cheap suit, and now she was playing me like Joe Average. I wanted to curse her ass out and hang up the phone, but I was too curious about what else she had to say.

"So, are we still going to get together to go out?" she asked.

"What did you have in mind?"

I could hear her take a deep breathe before responding.

"Well, how about taking me out for drinks at Bennigan's and then to dinner at Red Lobster."

I almost hit the ceiling. Not only did this woman ask me to take her out for drinks, but she had the audacity to request dinner too. All this after she waited damn near two weeks to call me. "This woman must be crazy," I thought to myself. I had other plans for her. After debating the point back and forth for about a half hour, I convinced her to come by for fried catfish and a bottle of white wine. At least that's what I told her.

When she arrived at 8:30 p.m., I had everything ready. A plate of hamburgers, a bowl of potato chips, and a cheap bottle of TJ Swann. She complained at first, but she was too hungry to turn down even that modest meal. Within fifteen minutes, her plate was clean and her glass was empty. I had never seen a woman eat like that before. You would've thought it was the last meal on earth. As the alcohol started to take effect, I decided to break out the hard stuff. I had a pitcher of jungle juice left over from a bachelor party earlier that week. For those of you who have never heard of jungle juice, it is a mixture of fresh fruit juices, clear liquors, and grain alcohol. When blended properly, it tastes like fruit punch or Kool-Aid. But don't let the sweet taste fool you, it will get you seriously fucked up.

I pulled out the tallest glass I could find and filled it to the brim. Without even asking what it was, she drank every drop of it. And the more she drank, the more the real Jennifer came out. Her proper speech became increasingly ghetto. Not because of the alcohol either, it was clearly a result of her inability to maintain her front.

"Jason, I cain't believe you didn't take me out to dunner," she slurred. "Nobody turns me down, not with this body."

By 10:30, I had lost what little respect I had for her. She was drinking like a fish and stumbling over my nice furniture. And to add insult to injury, she began taking inventory of my apartment.

"You have a nice place here," she said while inspecting my expensive paintings. "I bet you don't have any problems balancing your check book."

These remarks only added to my hostility since she still hadn't made any attempt to get to know me personally. That's right, men have feelings too. As the night went on, I began to feel more like an animal on a hunt than a man on a date. I was deviously waiting for a moment of weakness to move in for the kill. "One wrong move," I thought, "and your ass is mine." But believe it or not, I backed off. My mother did not raise her son to take advantage of women. Besides, who wants to have sex with an alcoholic? Not me! I may have been a little upset and disappointed, but I'm no sex maniac.

I stopped serving her drinks, and put on a pot of coffee. There was no way in the world she was driving home in her condition. I had to sober her up. While the coffee brewed, I started clearing away the dishes and wiping off the table. She politely moved out of my way and into the living room. I put on my favorite jazz station and opened the patio window to allow the cool breeze to flow through the apartment. For the next 20 minutes, she laid quietly on the sofa listening to the soft music. I couldn't believe she kept her mouth shut for that long. When the coffee was ready, I poured a cup and joined her on the sofa.

"Here, drink this," I said while handing her the hot cup.

"Thank you Jason, you are so sweet."

"You're welcome."

"I'm so embarrassed by the way I acted. Can you ever forgive me?"

"We'll see, just finish drinking your coffee."

The fresh air and the caffeine was definitely doing her some good. She sat up straight and began to speak more clearly. I decided to salvage what was left of this disastrous evening by showing her my vacation pictures and telling a few jokes. She listened attentively, and occasionally smiled to acknowledge my bad humor. And for a brief moment she reminded me of the provocative woman who I met at the card party. A very brief moment!

Shortly after midnight, I began straightening up around the apartment and washing the dinnerware, it was time to say good night. That's when she made the terrible mistake of sizing me up for "Sugar Daddy Duty." As I put away the dishes, she came into the kitchen to check my qualifications.

"By the way Jason, how is your credit?"

"Excuse me!"

She walked up behind me, pressed her breasts against my back, and elaborated.

"I was just curious because I'm trying to buy this new car and I need a co-signer."

My immediate reaction was to slap myself on the forehead with my soapy hand. I couldn't believe she had the nerve to form her mouth to say those words. "This woman is truly out of her damned mind," I thought. She had to go.

"Jennifer, do me a favor and go get your coat," I said. "I think it's time for you to leave."

"Why are men so tight?" she said while sliding her hand down between the sink and my crotch. "If I was your woman and needed help, wouldn't you be there for me? I mean, what if I was fifty dollars short on my rent or something?"

That was the last straw. I wiped the suds off my hands, rushed to the closet, and pulled out her jacket.

"Let's go Jennifer," I said while showing her the door. "Your time and your mind have expired."

"Come on Jason," she whined. "I'll be a good girl. Just let me stay with you tonight. I'm not ready to go home yet."

"You don't have to go home, but you've got to get the hell out of here!"

With that I slammed the door in her face, turned out the lights, and went to bed.

Of course, this was not the last dream date that turn into a nightmare. As recently as last month, I experienced another doozy. A woman who I had met at a networking party called me to invite me out to dinner. Remember, I did say she invited me out. Since she took the initiative to arrange the date, I volunteered to drive. I picked her up at 8:00, and we were on our way. When we arrived at the restaurant our table was waiting. To make a long story short, the food was great and the conversation was even better. After finishing our meal and having a glass of wine, she was ready to go. I left a generous tip on the table and we walked towards the register. As we approached the lobby area, I stopped to help her on with her coat, and then I excused myself to go to the bathroom. When I came out, she was standing at the register still holding the bill in her hand.

"Do you need help with change?" I asked.

"No, I'm waiting for you to pay for dinner."

"Here we go again," I angrily thought. "Different woman, same old game." I was so enraged that I stormed out of the restaurant, got in my car, and left her butt stranded. I couldn't believe she expected me to pay. Not half the bill, mind you, but the entire balance. Like I said, women are all the same. They're only interested in what a man can do for them. Well, two can play at that game.

The life of a nice guy is a difficult one. He lives in a world filled with women who don't appreciate his generosity or sensitivity. If he buys gifts and loans money he is viewed as gullible. And if he says, "I love you," and cries on his girlfriend's shoulder then he is a childish wimp. After years of being misunderstood and kicked to the curb he begins to feel the pressure to measure up to the macho, cold-hearted, playboy image. And with the help of an unfaithful wife or girlfriend, he is often pushed over the edge. Keith, who is a 21 year old college student, recently caught his girlfriend involved in extra-curricular activity. Since then, his attitude towards women has become very bitter, especially toward his girlfriend. "How could she do me like this?" he asks passionately. "If she wanted to fuck somebody else she should have ended our relationship." At a very young age he is learning what so many other men have as they mature, "Everything that glitters isn't gold."

> My mother always taught me to treat women with respect. She also taught me that if a man is honest with his woman he will receive the same in return. But my mother never met anyone like Cynthia. She turned out to be a real heartbreaker. We met at city college two years ago. The moment I laid eyes on her in the cafeteria, I knew she was the one for me. She had hazel green eyes, a beautiful smile, and wonderful sense of humor. And because she ran track, her body was in perfect condition. What a package! But the problem with this perfect package was how appealing it was to the other guys on campus. They wanted to unwrap it as much as I did. As it turned out, she had been unwrapped and test driven several times before and during our relationship.
>
> For the first twelve months we were together, life was great. Cynthia and I went to concerts, plays, and amusement parks. You name it, we did it. However, the following year was not so pleasant. I was accepted at a University in Atlanta, and she was staying here in Chicago. I thought the distance might cause a problem between us, so I sat down with her and discussed having an open relationship.

"Look Cynthia, I'm going to be away for three and four months at a time. I'll understand it if you want to see other guys while I'm gone."

"Is that really what you want, Keith?" she said sounding upset.

"Not really, but you are an attractive young woman and I know these guys are going to be sweating you left and right."

"Why don't you let me worry about that. I'm a big girl, and I can handle myself. But are you sure this idea of breaking up isn't for your benefit?"

"You know better than that baby. I only wanted to give you an opportunity to call it quits without any guilty feelings."

"Well, don't do me any favors," she said as her eyes began to swell up with tears. "I know what I want, and it's you."

This was exceptionally good news for me because I loved this young woman and wanted desperately to be her first love. I had been waiting patiently for two years and I wanted to be rewarded.

During the first three months of school, Cynthia and I talked every other day on the phone. But after only three months, three times a week turned into twice a week and then twice a month. I didn't think much about it because mid-term exams were kicking my ass. And besides, Christmas break was coming up and we knew we would be together again. The day of my last test, I called Cynthia and told her when to expect me home. I couldn't afford air fare so I decided to ride up with some friends who lived in Chicago. They were going to drop me off on Christmas Eve and pick me up the day after New Years. Everything was set, until the guy who's car I was supposed to ride in had an accident the day we were going to leave. "How bad can your luck get?" I asked myself. Of course, I had to call Cynthia with the bad news. She seemed very upset and disappointed that I couldn't make it. The emphasis is on the word *seemed*. As I sat in my dormitory room just about ready to cry, good old Dad came through with air fare. I was so excited about leaving, I forgot to call Cynthia. "She's going to be surprised!" I thought. And as it turned out, she was.

Once my plane landed, I thought about catching a taxi. But one look at the heavy traffic and my meager funds and I was easily persuaded to take the $1.50 train ride into town. I followed the signs to the CTA train station under the airport and hopped aboard the crowded cars. The ride to downtown was 35 minutes, so I killed time by day dreaming about Cynthia. "Man, it's going to feel good to hold her again," I envisioned. "And who knows, maybe she'll even give me some pussy for Christmas." Once I snapped out of my horny fantasy, I became more concerned about how lonely she must have been without me. Her mother was out of town on business and her best friend was spending the day with her boyfriend's family. I knew she would be all alone in her basement apartment with no one to keep her company. "It's Super Keith to the rescue," I joked to myself.

When the train reached my stop, I battled my way through the heavy crowd and headed straight for the florist. By the time I got there all of the red roses had been sold out, so I bought a long stem yellow rose and a beautiful card instead. After all, it's the thought that counts. When I arrived at her place, I peeked into the living room window hoping to startle her. But all I saw was a bottle of beer on the table and one of her night gowns on the floor. Although Cynthia hated alcohol, I didn't think much of it. I decided to go around back to knock on her bedroom window. "She's really going to be shocked," I thought. But what happened next shocked only me. As I tiptoed around to the rear, I began to hear faint sounds of a thumping and squeaking. The closer I got, the louder it became. "Squeak, thump, squeak, thump!" Somebody was getting busy, and I mean real busy. Once I made it completely around to her window, it was clear where those sounds were coming from.

"Whose is it, whose is it?" a man's voice asked forcefully.

"It's yours baby, it's yours." Cynthia's exhausted voice submitted.

"Is it good baby, is it good?"

"Yes, baby it's good. Don't stop, please don't stop."

My heart dropped to the ground. Here I was playing the perfect gentleman role, waiting patiently for her to be ready. And come to find out she was ready all along. "Why didn't she just tell me?" I cried inside. I was willing to let her pursue other relationships. But no! She elected to hold out on me, and sleep with everybody else on the side. As I stood there in total shock, I pulled out my pen and wrote her a quick message on the card I bought.

Dear Cynthia,

Today you broke my heart. I came home to surprise you, but it was me who got the surprise. For years I was fooled into believing your body was priceless, a Bloomingdales exclusive. But as I have finally found out, it is worthless, nothing more than flea market overstock. Nevertheless, I would like to say, "Thank you." Thank you for screwing me and the man you were with today, although I'm sure he got more enjoyment out of it than I did. But most importantly, thank you for a special kind of education about trusting women. It is one that I will carry with me for the rest of my life.

P.S. Let this flower be a reminder of how sweet and caring a man I used to be.

Signed,

No More Mr. Nice Guy

Many women will argue that men being hurt in relationships have nothing to do with infidelity. But it is clear to me from listening to a number of these cases, that the effects can be devastating. Again, let me emphasize that true relationships are built on trust. And if that trust is damaged, whether it be today or ten years ago, the man will be hesitant to trust or love again. Some people may call it shielding, immaturity, or even insecurity. The point is he will do whatever it takes to keep from being vulnerable again. And while he's about the business of shielding, getting even, or whatever you want to call it, guess who's getting hurt? That's right, the innocent woman who had absolutely nothing to do with his bad experiences. Of course, the vengeful man is unwilling to stop his onslaught long enough to take this into account. In his mind, everyone must pay. The women who have hurt him in the past and those who might play games with him in the future. However, this type of mentality is destructive and only serves to create a vicious cycle of manipulation and humiliation. The resentful man takes advantage of a particular woman, she in turn finds a man to get even with. Where will it all end?

NOTHIN' BUT THE DOG IN ME

If there was ever a time to break out the Purina Dog Chow and Sergeant flea collars this would be it. What examination of the cheating man would be complete without a long hard look at the infamous D-O-G? As one woman so eloquently put it, "Any man who cheats is a dog, atomic dog, under dog, mighty dog, and last but not least, deputy dog." Now, after you have collected yourselves off the floor from laughter, we can look deeper into the mind of this pathological sex addict. To begin with, he has a chauvinistic and barbaric perception of women. In his mind, they are merely sexual objects put on this earth for the sole purpose of satisfying his lustful appetite. Forget about compassion, humor, and intellect. Those qualities are unnecessary for the duties he needs performed. As one man boldly stated, "A Nobel Prize and Ph.d won't be of much use when the woman is lying on her back."

The dog cheating man is a habitual liar who has mastered the art of insensitivity. While looking his wife or girlfriend squarely in the eyes, he can say, "I Love you," and then sleep with her best friend without an ounce of guilt. To put it frankly, he can marry you on Sunday and screw the bridesmaids on Monday. And what does the dog have to say in his defense? Not a damned thing! He is a cold-hearted, selfish-minded, menace to female society who makes no apologies for his conduct. As a matter of fact, he actually believes that his services are vital to the community. In the words of one Dog, "If every man chose to remain monogamous, the world would be full of women with 24 hour PMS and bad skin."

This impudent remark is just one of many examples of how crude and insensitive the Dog can truly be. He has an ego the size of the Grand Canyon and a little black book that resembles the yellow pages. Women are merely numbers with notches placed by their names to indicate level of sexual performance, orally and otherwise. The act of sex has no emotional significance in his life. It is nothing more than recreational sport and a dispassionate game of tag to pass the time away. Nevertheless, the D-O-G receives all of the attention and acclaim from television talk show hosts and journalists. Without consideration for any other motivating factors, he is held up as the one who best represents all of cheating mankind. For the purpose of this chapter, so be it!

"A woman's legs, breasts, hips, and lips are just too much for any mortal man to resist," says 35 year old Ron. He has been divorced for three years and says that his natural desire to be with other women is too overwhelming to control. In his own words, "Men are warriors who must venture out and conquer pussy, it's that simple." Well, it's quite obvious this guy won't receive any awards for deep intellectual thought. However, you must admit his statement is typical of how most men really think. They see themselves as animals trying to be spiritual, when in fact they are spiritual beings fighting against their animalistic selves, or flesh. This is the distinct characteristic of the Dog. He is a self-proclaimed beast who is unwilling to elevate himself above slavishly primitive behavior.

Understanding the Dog is as simple as 1-2-3. One, he has no regard for the feelings of anyone's except his own. Two, he will do whatever it takes to get his victim into bed. And three, the Dog proceeds with his sexual assault on women simply because he loves the game. And I mean LOVE! How does the song go? "Can't get enough, of that funky stuff!" This is his National Anthem, his motto, his mentality. Forget about negative role models. This guy has made a conscious choice to have as many women as humanly possibly. Of course, I'm still referring to 35 year old Ron. He is the epitome of the cheating Dog.

Since childhood he hasn't been able to keep his hands off of the girls. While the other little boys were out playing baseball and basketball, he was organizing a game of Spin the bottle and Catch a girl kiss a girl.

As an adult, he has never managed to remain monogamous for more than two months at a time. Which obviously explains why he's divorced. The controversy surrounding Ron had nothing to do with his lack of sexual control but his unwillingness to accept 100% of the responsibility for his behavior. Can you believe this guy? He actually had the audacity to blame women for at least half of his dogish deeds. What does he mean by that, you ask? Don't ask me. Let's get it straight from the horse's mouth or should I say, "Straight from the pound?"

> First of all, I resent the term "Dog" to describe what is simply a choice of lifestyle. I choose to have several women, it's that simple. In my opinion this is the only sane way to carry on with relationships. No commitment, no worries, and no headaches. I can come and go as I please, no questions asked. Sure, I may have to lie every now and then to keep the peace, but women expect that anyway. I just keep my business undercover so nobody gets hurt. Now before you get the idea I'm being cold-blooded about this whole monogamy thing, let me explain something to you. I've tried to be faithful on a number of occasions, but I just can't do it. No matter how attractive and sexually satisfying the woman is, sooner or later I get bored.
>
> Like most men, I need a little variety and excitement in my life. And having sex with different women provides me with both. There's no feeling in the world that can compare to meeting a beautiful woman and then taking her to bed. You get a rush as she unsnaps her bra

and pulls off her pants for the first time. It's kind of like Christmas and New Years rolled up into one night. First you unwrap the gift, then you celebrate until the break of dawn. I know this may sound raunchy, but it's real. I love the idea of laying in bed with a tender young thang on Friday and waking up next to an experienced vet on Saturday. After all, a man needs more than one pair of shoes to wear, right? A pair for jogging, a pair for work, and a dress pair. Women are no different. You've got to be able to mix it up a bit.

The most upsetting thing about being a so-called Dog is listening to other men beg and kiss women's asses just to get into their pants. They use stupid lines such as, "Sex isn't everything, you know. I prefer a woman who has something to offer intellectually." Fuck that! I'll take a good blow job over a spelling Bee any day. The only academic requirements I insist on are basic reading and writing skills. If she can scribble her phone number on a napkin, and decipher the street address to my apartment, she's a rocket scientist as far as I'm concerned.

Then you have these hypocritical married men who stand on their matrimonial soap boxes preaching monogamy. They brag about how wonderful married life is and try to convince you to settle down. But those are usually the same horny bastards who end up on the ten o'clock news getting busted with some hooker named Trixy at motel Scum Bucket. The truth of the matter is, all men have a little dog in them. If they had the opportunity to lay down with a sexy woman without being found out, most of them would do it without a second thought. I don't know of any man in his right mind who cherishes the idea of having sex with only one women for the rest of his life. If he tells you he does, he's either lying or impotent.

Now let me explain what I meant by women being responsible in part for my behavior. To begin with, I think they should take a long hard look at just how provocatively they dress when leaving the house. Todays fashions can make even the most innocent choir girl look like a whore. "How does that relate to men being dogs?" you ask. Allow me to explain. Women have begun to dress in ways that put more emphasis on what they have to offer downstairs as opposed to upstairs. I can go anywhere downtown, during business hours mind you, and see women walking around with half of their behind showing and their nipples sticking through their blouses. And these same women will have the nerve to ask, "What are you looking at?" And "Why are men so dogish?" Give me a break! Women know men are only human. If they truly wanted us to stop acting like dogs, they would make more of an effort to cover up those delicious looking bones.

Women also have the nerve to expect men to be 100% honest about their marital status. But again, their attire makes it virtually impossible. How can any mortal man resist lying when he is approached by a woman wearing a pair of daisy duke shorts, a fresh paint job, and a tight halter top with her tits showing? "Do you have a girlfriend?" they ask. "Are you married?" One look at her small waist, thick thighs, and those 36 D's and he's going to instantly become the most eligible bachelor in America. Even the most loyal of men have been known to crack under the pressure of a beautiful face and a pair of large breasts. The fact that he has a wife, two children, and a dog named Spot at home does-n't even cross his mind until after she asks for his phone number. "Selective Amnesia," I call it.

Revealing clothing isn't the only reason why I feel women contribute to infidelity. The Dogs like my friends and I are bombarded daily with examples of how lonely and desperate women are. So desperate in fact, that I recently saw a program where a woman was married to herself. Now, tell me there isn't a need for the dog to pitch in. Women have bought completely into the "Male Shortage Theory," which is perfectly fine with us. We love to watch talk shows like Oprah Winfrey, Phil Donahue, and Ricki Lake. They have dedicated hundreds of hours to finding eligible men for overly anxious women. Some of these guys had been shipped in from Alaska, Scotland, Ireland, and probably from Disneyland for all I know. And what type of message do you think this sends to the so-called Dogs of the world? I'll tell you what the message is, "Feeding time!"

So, as you can see, female society needs us Dogs. Who else can be counted on to promptly answer their desperate call to be seen, caressed, and stroked the right way? And what's more impressive, we don't discriminate. Full figured, short, tall, we love them all. One buddy of mine, for example, will date a short, slim woman on Friday, and turn right back around and tackle a 6 ft. 250 pounder on Saturday. As he put it, "I don't mind a light weight every now and then, but I prefer a woman with a little meat on her bones." Then you have the very educated and undersexed woman of the 90s. She lays in bed alone most every weekend staring endlessly at the mantel filled with degrees and academic awards. All the while her arms and body ache, unnecessarily, for the love or lust of a real man. If only she would consider giving a man like myself a chance. I have a

Masters degree in Economics and a Ph.d in Longevity. Now that's what I call appealing to her intellect.

And to all of you married women out there I say, "Get off your hypocritical high horse!" You know how valuable a service we have rendered to your group. Time after time we have come through to save the day whenever there has been a deficiency on the home front. Answer these questions honestly. When your husbands have come up a little short, who is it that saves the day with a few more inches? The Dog! When you get tired of having his fat stomach crushing your intestines, who is it that provides you with a nice firm body to jump up and down on, all night long? The Dog! And finally, when your man refuses to take a dive between your thighs, who is it that goes down below where he won't go? The Dog! With that in mind, the only question I have left is, "Have you hugged a dog today?"

While most men are unquestionably motivated by the sexual pleasures of cheating, there is another factor which seems to be just as significant. That is the pure emotional and psychological excitement of sleeping with different women. I label this type of Dog as the Egomaniac. This scoundrel is often more concerned with being admired than getting laid. He is an arrogant, self-absorbed, wanna be playboy who must be constantly reminded of how great he is. Paul, who is 45 years old, fits this description perfectly. He admits that his periodic affairs play an important part in how he identifies with himself. In his words, "Being able to attract a beautiful young woman makes me feel good about myself. As long as I can charm the pants off of them, I'll never grow old." Well, I don't know about that, but he made one hell of an impression on one young lady.

The last time I polished up on my gigolo skills was two month ago while on a business trip. I met this very attractive flight attendant on my way back from Phoenix. While she was serving peanuts and coffee, I was serving up the old charm. By the time we landed in New York, she was hooked. She wrote down her home phone number, pager number, address, and bra size. When I called her a couple of days later, she didn't waste any time getting straight to the point. "I'm attracted to older men," she admitted. "And I would like to get to know you better." Needless to say, she got to know me very well. Since she had four other flight attendants sharing her apartment, we reserved a room at a motel outside of the city. The moment we walked through the door, she reached inside her small suitcase for something comfortable to slip into. I caught a quick peek at what looked like a tiny bra held together with dental floss.

"Oh my God," I said. "Are you going to put that skimpy thing on?"

"Stop looking," she said while shielding it from my view. "You're going to spoil the surprise."

"Baby, I don't think anything could spoil that surprise, especially with a body like yours."

She blushed and headed for the bathroom with her bag of goodies.

"I'll be back," she said seductively.

Once she closed the door, I went into action. First I took my clothes off and folded them neatly on the chair. Then I used the sink outside of the bathroom to touch myself up a bit. Just in case you ladies didn't know it, men are notorious for washing their dicks in the sink. Finally, I got down on the floor and did 50 push-ups. I wanted to be buffed for my new lover. The second the shower shut off, I leaped onto the bed and did my best to look athletic.

"Are you ready baby?" she said as the bathroom door swung open.

"Ready like Freddy," I laughed.

When she walked out into the open, all the blood rushed out of one head and into the other. She had on a crotchless black lace teddy, with garter straps, and high heel pumps. I was in heaven. For the next two hours we did it in every position humanly possible. On top of the sink, in the shower, and against the wall. When it was all over, she collapsed on the bed and fell asleep. I just laid there staring at her thinking to myself, "Another first round knockout. I've still got it!"

At 45 years of age, I know many women will criticize me for not conducting myself more responsibly, especially since I'm well educated with a professional job. However, being a Dog has nothing to do with economics or intellect. Don't fool yourselves for a moment into believing this is some sort of low income or low education thing. It's simply a man thing. Discussion about sordid affairs take place at exclusive health clubs, on the 16th hole of golf courses, and even after church on Sunday. That's right, the Dogs are everywhere. Cheating is a universal game played by men from every social, economic, and cultural background. As a matter of fact, I have seen more infidelity in corporate America than in the ghetto.

The executives on my job, for example, screw around more than any men I've ever seen. The vice president in charge of marketing is my favorite to watch. He is 54 years old and has been married for over twenty five

> years. Nevertheless, he loves to show off his prize catch, just like a cocky high school kid. Without an ounce of shame, he allows his mistress to come upstairs to the office to pick him up for lunch. And she always has on a sexy outfit. I'm thoroughly convinced he insists she wear something provocative simply to shock the rest of the staff. When they first began dating three months ago, she was dressed very business like and conservatively. Now she appears to have raided Cher's wardrobe. Last week she stepped off of the elevator wearing a suede mini skirt, a see-through blouse, and four inch pumps. I had to roll my tongue back into my head. And you should see him when he returns from their lunch dates. He struts around with his chest all pushed out like a peacock. This may all seem very juvenile from a woman's perspective, but some men need to use attractive women to feel good about themselves, including me. I guess the old saying is true, "You can't teach an old Dog new tricks."

The cheating man's sexual and egotistical need for dogging women is often nothing more than a clever camouflage of the larger problem of insecurity. The problem, however, was finding a man willing to discuss this topic from that perspective. After all, it's not easy to walk up to a grown man and say "Excuse me Sir, I'm writing a book about infidelity, and I need a man who is insecure to tell me his side of the story." I don't think so. How many men do you think would actually admit to being insecure? One in five? One in a hundred perhaps? Try one in a million. When it comes to examining infidelity from this particular point of view, most men get awfully touchy. Why? Because "Insecurity" is a word synonymous with weakness and femininity. And I don't need to tell you how offensive those words can be to a **real** man. The trick now was to come up with a word, or term which would address the issue of insecurity, without calling it insecurity. I thought about it for a moment, then it came to me, "I'll call it 'Back Up.'" And just as I expected, they took to this term like fish to water.

The cheating man's need for "Back Up," is based primarily on control. But it also has a great deal to do with fear. First let's examine the control motive. Most men, regardless if they are cheating or not, have an inherent, conditioned, and often whimsical need to be in control. Of course, this is not a problem if he simply wants to change the light bulb, try unsuccessfully to fix the family car, or drive around the block lost for an hour. However, when matters of the heart are at issue, the idea of control cannot be dealt with by using a socket wrench or a road map. This is a major concern for the post Neanderthal man who has been accustomed to having a solution to every physical problem. The key word of course is physical, not emotional.

Sure, he's willing to submit to the mechanical expertise of a repair man if he can't start his car, or ask the gas attendant for directions when he is lost. But who does he call when his relationship isn't working and he feels lost in it? His buddies? His Mommy? Or a therapist perhaps? Are you crazy! No man with an ounce of pride is going to surrender himself to the embarrassment of his friends, the scrutiny of his mother, or the nosiness of some pencil neck therapist. In his mind, there is only one way to effectively maintain control over his relationship. And that is simply not to get too seriously, or emotionally involved in it. As one gentleman candidly put it, "The one who is least in love usually controls the relationship."

It is because of this type of mentality that more and more men are subscribing to the 90s doctrine that states: "Never love a woman more than you love yourself." Sounds harmless, right? WRONG! For the defensive and emotionally apprehensive man, this philosophy translates to, "I will not allow myself to get so intimately involved that I might lose control over my relationship." Does this sound familiar? Sure it does. The cheating man's interpretation is skewed only because he is constantly looking for a reason not to love anyway. However, if we had presented this slogan to a woman and turned it around to read: "Never love a man more than you love yourself," she would have likely comprehended this to mean, "I will love and care for my man, but I will take time out for myself too." Sadly, this is one of the many classic examples of just how differently men and women think. The woman is always prepared to love again, no matter how many times her battle ridden heart has been broken. Whereas the man treats love like a Jehovah's witness knocking at the door, hoping it will go away if he draws the curtains to his heart and keeps quiet.

The issue of fear is another dominant factor as to why men feel the need for "Back Up." Fear of what you ask? The fear of falling in love, that's what. Many men will strongly disagree with this remark simply because they have no idea what it's like to be close enough to a woman to give a damn. They passionately deny any woman could ever hurt them. While at the same time they are too afraid to get close enough to give it a try. "What are we afraid of?" you ask. The unknown. The canine cheating man has a corny and over exaggerated idea of what love is all about. Subconsciously he is afraid that once he falls in love, he will be instantly transformed into a mindless, spineless, pussy whipped robot who will lose complete control over his life. Therefore he will remain in his comfort zone where the emotional territory is familiar and controllable. That of course, is the land of lies and deceit.

As for the cheating man who has tried love before, he is too chicken hearted and paranoid to surrender to the goddess of love again. Any woman who threatens to get too close, immediately reminds him of the dark days. That horrible period when Mr. Debonair lost his mystical powers and was transformed into Mr. Sensitive. When he was unable to depend on the childish rap of a playboy and was forced to rely on the mature communication skills of an adult. In those days he was equally vulnerable and hated every minute of it. All men are secretly guarding against having these experiences. This of course, is why many of us steer clear of any woman who represents true affection and strong commitment.

It's kind of painfully funny when you think about it. With all of our bulging muscles and bold talk we cannot handle emotional injury half as well as women can. Some say it's because women have had much more painful practice, while others contend it's nothing more than social conditioning. Well, I have my own theory, "Men are simply more sensitive than women are to begin with." I know all hell is going to break loose when my male peers get a load of that statement. No matter, I'm going to stick by my guns on this one.

Before we allow sleeping dogs to lay, there is one last story I would like to share with you. It is an insightful look at how one man covered up his insecurities, and or fears, by keeping as many women as possible on hand. The name of this interesting fellow is Maurice. He is single, conceited, and has 29 years of experience to certify his Dog License. What I found most interesting about him, was the way in which he viewed his relationships with women. He expressed his attitude about cheating with a very colorful basketball analogy. The women are going to scream foul on this one.

> I look at my relationships with women like a game of basketball. I'm the coach and they are the players. The first order of business for the coach is to find a star

player, a woman to build the team around. She will be expected to come through under pressure, night in and night out. Her responsibilities will include coming to all practice sessions and scoring on a consistent basis. If she performs up to standards, her contract will be renegotiated and she will be allowed to stay with the team indefinitely. Then you have your two back up players who are also expected to perform well. They are a very integral part of the team since the starter can't be expected to come through 30 consecutive days, if you know what I mean. Finally, you have your two bench warmers. Although they may not get much starting time, don't sell them short. In a pressure situation, they will give you everything they've got. Recruiting such a cohesive unit is no easy task. You must be willing to travel all across town to find the perfect combination. That includes wedding receptions, bowling alleys, and even funerals. No place is off limits to a coach who is determined to win.

All jokes aside, I feel it is absolutely necessary to keep as many women on stand-by as possible. This is the only way I can put up with all the games women play in this society. What do I mean by that? Well, allow me to run it down to you. Let's start with the average date. You call a woman up, drive fifty miles across town to pick her up, spend all your money, and then drive her back home, right? Wrong! I don't play that. My attitude is this, "Either we're fucking or you can stay at home." I'm not going to allow a woman to come by my apartment, eat me out of house and home, and watch Blockbuster videos all night. I can do that by myself.

Another reason why I need to have more than one woman is because women can sense when a man is hard up, like Latoya Jackson 1-900-Psychic or something. Those tramps at the night club are the worst. They sit back with their noses all turned up acting as if Fabio or Denzel Washington is waiting at home with champagne and flowers. When they know damn well the only welcome home they're going to get is from Fi Fi the poodle and Morris the cat. Nevertheless, these lonely heifers play you like Joe Sausage Head. Without any consideration for how much you can afford to spend, they start making demands on your wallet. "Buy me a drink." "Take me out to breakfast." And the ultimate insult, "Help me out with my rent." Now tell me, do you think a man who has a big booty, firm breasted, toe licking nymphomaniac waiting at home in his bed would put up with these requests? Hell no! And that's exactly why I need my back up crew. So I can tell any woman who wants to be wined and dined, to kiss my ass.

But being a dog is not always about having a woman in your bed. As a matter of fact, I spend most of my time alone. I work 10 hours a day, play basketball three times a week, and take care of my daughter most every weekend. With such a busy schedule you can understand why I don't have time for games. When a woman comes over to my place, it's all about the business. Of course, the regular players are trained for on the spot sex but the new ones can sometimes present a problem. A young lady I recently met at a concert is the perfect example of why I need back up. Her name was Valerie. For two weeks she called me on the phone boasting about how she was going to turn me out and make my nose bleed. But on the night we finally got together, she was whistling a different tune.

She arrived at my place at 11:00 wearing a pair of cut

off shorts and a tank top. I escorted her straight to the bedroom and threw my tongue down her throat. Within seconds we were rolling on the bed feeling all over each other. When things really started to heat up, I made my move by unsnapping her shorts. Now, guess what her reaction was after talking all that shit on the phone. She grabbed my hand, pushed me away and said, "I need more time to get to know you better before we have sex." I wanted to curse her dick teasing ass out. But instead, I kept my cool and took the opportunity to give her an education about men.

"Look Valerie, I'm sexually attracted to you and you're obviously sexually attracted to me, so what's with all the games?"

"I just want to get more comfortable with you, that's all," she whined. "I only met you two weeks ago and I hardly know anything about you. We haven't really talked about a relationship or even gone out anywhere together."

"Let me tell you something baby, I don't have the time or financial resources to see you every week or take you out a hundred times before we become intimate. And besides, this idea you women have of getting to know a man better is the most ridiculous thing I've ever heard."

"Why do you say that?"

"Because a man will never show you his true self until after he's been getting the sex on a regular basis. And then he still may never reveal himself."

After I delivered my speech, I politely walked her to the door and kicked her frigid butt out. My best friend Randy told me I was in the wrong and should've been more patient. However, he was more sympathetic two nights later when the same thing happened to him. A woman he met at a night club came over to his apartment at 1:00 a.m. dressed in a pair of biker shorts and a bikini top. She kissed him, grind him, and asked him to suck her breast. But when he tried to lead her into the bedroom she pretended to be upset and threatened to leave. And since Randy is one of those nice guys who doesn't believe in back up, he had to put up with her game playing and teasing all night long.

Again, I don't have that problem. If a particular woman can't play by my rules, I'll put her on waivers just like the NBA. There are always available women out there who will be more than willing to fill her slot. An unrestricted free agent, if you will. This process is known as "Drafting." There are plenty of good recruits out there too, if you know where to look. The grocery stores, for example, are great places to scout good rebounders. The laundromats, on the other hand, are prime locations to find that agile woman who can put it in the basket. Even church can be a great place to recruit if you're looking for an unselfish player who will pass the ball. The bottom line is this, I need a solid back-up crew in order to make my life more comfortable and secure. The only question is, What do I call this team? How about the Seattle Standbys, or the Atlanta Alternates? I Just Love This Game!

Now that playtime is over, let us turn our attention to the more serious and less publicized examination of the so-called decent cheating man who has also strayed away from home. Revered as the most honest, trustworthy, and family oriented of them all, he, too, has needs. Needs which aren't being met at home, for whatever reasons. But unlike the D-O-G, he is not deliberately seeking out women for sexual conquests. In his case, intercourse is nothing more than a subsequential act between two people who have found other interests and worthwhile goals in common. In other words, sex is often the unexpected result, not the motivating factor. Now before you men out there start beating your chests and slapping five over that assessment, consider this. Although these explanations for cheating are much less cruel and vengeful, they are nevertheless just as painful for the wife or girlfriend who eventually finds out.

EVERYTHING I MISS AT HOME

"Home Sweet Home." "Home is where the heart is." And last but not least, "A man's home is his castle." These are very touching phrases used to express the attitude of the man who is looking forward to coming home to his woman. He may not necessarily live in a mansion or have a perfect life, but he has a roof over his head and his needs are being met. But what about the man whose needs aren't being met? What does he have to look forward to? Those catchy phrases mean little or nothing to him since he is often neglected, disrespected, and misunderstood. From his point of view, home is not sweet, but sour. And as for his noble castle, it may just as well be a ragged Hobo's shack. Because unless the queen is performing her royal duties, the King is unhappy and unfulfilled. What are these so-called "duties?" you ask. Well, at the risk of being labeled a male chauvinist, I would have to say there are basically three. One of which is satisfying the man's egotistical needs. Men are overgrown babies who must have their egos stroked in order to be happy. They need to be told on a consistent basis just how intelligent, handsome, and wonderful they are, whether it's the truth or not.

Another important responsibility of the wife or girlfriend, is to see to the intellectual and supportive needs of her man. If a man makes a conscious effort to educate himself or simply get ahead in life, he deserves a woman who will appreciate his ambition. One who is totally committed to standing by his side through thick and thin. The so-called independent woman of the 90s has no staying power. At the first sign of trouble, she is packed and ready to move on to the next sucker. Finally, there is the vital issue of the man's sexual needs. Aside from long tiresome work days, menstrual cramps, and other feminine problems, the man expects his woman to be sexually available to him 24 hours a day, 7 days a week. The last thing he needs is a mate who is never ready, and is rationing out sex as if the supply was limited. This is an area where most men are unwilling to compromise, and must have absolute satisfaction, or else! "Or else what?" you ask. Or else he may decide to seek the affection of another woman who is more willing to give him what he wants, when he wants it.

If a woman neglects or refuses to provide her man with these so-called basic needs, is he then justified in pursuing outside relationships? "Hell No!" say millions of women who are sick and tired of men using this weak excuse to justify their horny behavior. They believe men who feel dissatisfied at home should either talk it out, seek counseling, or leave the woman alone altogether. However, men know their choices aren't always so cut and dry. Other factors must be taken into consideration; ones which are emotionally draining and economically costly. A gentleman from Los Angeles typified my point.

"I've been married for ten years." he admits. "I can't just pack my suitcase, gas up the old Chevy, and drive off into the sunset. I have a mortgage to pay and two beautiful children who depend on me. Not only that, but my wife would take me to the cleaners in a California divorce."

After making a thorough evaluation of his domestic and financial situation, he has determined that his move would be both impossible and impractical. For the moment, he is trapped. He sincerely wants to leave, but can't. Now what? The cheating man, depending on the extent to which he is able to tolerate his subordinate position, must eventually make a decision. To leave or not to leave? Or rather, to cheat or not to cheat? That is the question.

Patrick, who is 29 years old, had to face this same dilemma a year ago. He became totally fed up with his wife's constant nagging and attempts at trying to change him. "While we were dating in college, she was fun loving and seemed to accept me for who I was," he says. "But after we got married and started to make good money, she became snobbish and expected me to act differently." However, Patrick was not that kind of man. He was raised in Detroit by a hard working, blue collar father who taught him to judge people by their human wealth not their net worth. His idea of a good time was watching basketball and drinking beer with his buddies. His wife Nicole, in contrast, was from a well to do family in New Orleans. She was basically a spoiled brat who fit in very well with the snobbish crowd. Watching basketball and sipping on beer was definitely not her cup of tea. A year after graduation, they both landed great jobs in Chicago and decided to get married. But after only one year of what seemed to be the perfect relationship, he found himself becoming deeply involved with another woman. Inquiring minds want to know, "What happened?"

> Our marriage started out like a fairy tale. We were both college graduates and very much in demand in our respective fields. And with combined salaries of $80,000, we were well on our way to living the American Dream. As it turned out, all that money could not buy a dime's worth of understanding and consideration. After getting settled in our new home, we began aggressively pursuing our careers. During those first twelve months, things were very hectic. Nicole was working sixty hours a week handling contracts and other paperwork for a government agency. Meanwhile, I was putting in long hours and routinely flying out of town on business. It got to the point where we hardly ever slept in the same bed together. How does the expression go? "Two ships passing in the night," that

was definitely us. We willingly accepted this chaotic lifestyle as the price to be paid for success. However, this did not go on forever. As our work loads began to lighten up, we spent more time together becoming better acquainted as husband and wife, and as human beings. But what I soon discovered was we weren't exactly on the same page, or even the same planet.

As the weeks and months rolled by, it was obvious Nicole had bought completely into the yuppie, corporate ideology. First she insisted on updating our wardrobes. "Something more sophisticated," she said. I went along with it. Then she wanted an expensive painting for the living room. I went along with that too. Finally, she decides we simply had to have a new automobile. Something that would be, in her words, "More reflective of our status." She managed to drag me down to the BMW dealership to purchase a brand new 1993 325si. Now, keep in mind we still had to make our $2,000 a month mortgage payments, and repay my student loan. I know $80,000 sounds like a lot of money, but it doesn't mean you're rich. Besides, I was perfectly content with my faded blue jeans, Michael Jordan posters, and trusty old Ford. "Who is she trying to impress anyway?" I wondered. But, since we didn't have any children or massive credit card bills, I didn't complain. "What the hell," I convincingly told myself. "We deserve to enjoy the fruits of our labor." It never dawned on me however, that the atmosphere and identity she was trying so hard to create was for her comfort and my exclusion. Sure, I was intelligent, handsome, and ambitious, but I just didn't have that attitude which says, "I'm better than you." Of course, she did.

Our differences were becoming more apparent with

the passing of each day, especially with regards to our choices of friends. Most of my associates were postmen, bus drivers, and guys who hung out at the gym. Nicole's friends, on the other hand, were real prima donnas. Her friend Tiffany was the biggest bitch of them all. She drove a Mercedes and always had her nose turned up. The difference in our social lives became even more evident when she refused to allow her friends to mix with mine. She never once invited them over to the house, at least not while I was around. But to be honest with you, I really didn't give a damn. My friends and I were having a ball, and the presence of her stuck up girlfriends would have only spoiled the mood anyway. What did bother me however, was the disrespectful and inconsiderate way in which she would greet my company at the door. Without even so much as a hello, she would turn her back and walk away after letting them in.

"He's downstairs," she would rudely say. "And don't forget to wipe your feet."

And then there were the never-ending sarcastic remarks regarding their economic status. My best friend, who just happened to be a plumber, was her favorite target.

"So, is Mr. Handy Man coming over tonight?" she wisely remarked.

"Yes he is. Why do you ask?"

"Could you ask him not to park his raggedy maintenance truck in front of the house?"

This was undoubtedly her smart ass way of attacking his blue collar profession. I guess she figured he wasn't intellectual enough for her taste. What's so ridiculously funny about her whole attitude is he damn near makes more money than both of us put together.

But that obviously didn't matter to her. He was a common laborer and she was above that.

Because I loved my wife and wanted to keep our relationship from drifting apart, I decided to sit down with her and openly discuss my concerns. I left work early, bought her favorite bottle of wine, and rushed home to cook. I wanted the mood to be just right. When she made it home at 5:30, a candlelight dinner was laid out on the dining room table. The wine was chilling and the curtains were drawn. She was clearly moved. I waited until after we were finished eating to tell her how I felt.

"Nicole, I don't like where our relationship is headed. We need to do something about spending more time together, more quality time. You are my wife and I love you, all I need is for you to meet me half way. How about it?"

As she listened to my words, tears began to fall from her eyes. "I feel the same way too sweetheart. Things are getting a little out of hand. Just tell me what you need me to do."

After talking it over for a couple of hours, we decided on two things. One, to take a vacation together in the Fall. Either a trip to Hawaii or a seven day Carnival cruise. Secondly, we agreed to throw a get acquainted party for all our friends. We figured this would be a great way to spend more recreational time together. All of this took place on a Friday evening in July. But it wasn't until late Sunday that we began making specific plans for the party. I remember that discussion vividly because it was a very hot and steamy night. And I'm not just talking about the temperature either. Her idea was to arrange a dinner party on a Friday evening. Of course, I preferred something less formal, like having a barbecue on a Saturday afternoon. What began as a civil discussion, turned into a very revealing argument.

"Look baby." I said. "This formal setting sounds very nice, but people don't want to be all cramped up when they're trying to get to know one another. After all, this is supposed to be pleasure, not business."

That's when she slammed her pen down on the table and gave me a look which I had never seen before.

"I wish I had never agreed to go along with this stupid idea in the first place!" she shouted. "I knew you weren't going to approve of anything that would make your simple-minded friends uncomfortable. Let's just forget the whole thing altogether."

"Damn! Where did that come from?"

"I'm sorry honey," she apologized. "It's hot and I'm tired, let's just go to bed."

She gave me a dispassionate hug, walked upstairs and got in the shower. As I began to turn off the lights, I stopped to sit down on the sofa to fully absorb all that was said. I realized then that her attack was as much directed at me as to my so-called "Simple minded" friends. Despite my good looks, education, and respectable position, my image was not polished enough to show off to her bourgeoisie friends. I had a strange feeling from that day on, things would never be quite the same between us. Unfortunately, I was right.

The weeks following that incident were filled with sly comments about my attire around the house, and how I spent my recreational time. One day she went too far. I was sitting on the living room sofa, minding my own business, when she walked in with an attitude.

"Why don't you put on that nice sports shirt and slacks I bought you? Don't you get tired of wearing gym shoes and jogging pants all the time?"

"Now she wants to play fashion consultant," I said under my breath.

I ignored her remarks and went back to watching my basketball game. I guess she got the message because she stormed out of the room with a frustrated look on her face. But she wasn't through yet. One hour later, she was back to pick up right where she left off.

"Why do you have to go play basketball with those same guys every weekend?" she rudely inquired. "Can't you spend some of your time over at the golf range instead?"

That was about all I could take from her. Trying to change my character and choose my friends was her worst mistake ever. I made one last effort to control my temper, but it was in vain.

"Let's get something straight!" I said while pointing my finger in her face. "I work hard every day. And if I choose to sit around this house all day buck naked, with a beer in my hand, that's my business. And furthermore, I don't want to hear anymore of your rich girl shit about who my friends are and stupid golf. Now leave me the hell alone and go play with your counterfeit Barbie Doll girl friends!"

She grabbed her purse off the counter, gave me a mean look and slammed the door shut. I was upset too, so I snatched my gym bag off the patio and jogged the half mile to the health club. I needed something to relax me, and the gym always seem to be the perfect medicine. On that particular day, it was exactly what the doctor ordered.

By the time I finished my routine and changed into my swim trunks, it was about 9:30 p.m. The club was going to be closing in a half hour. So, I dashed out of the shower and headed for the water. I was determined to get in a few laps before leaving. After splashing around like a mad man for about twenty minutes, I took a rest on the edge of the pool. That's when I looked up and noticed the aerobic class letting out. Jessica, who was one of the instructors, acknowledged me with a wave and began making her way down. What I liked about her was how polite and cheerful she always seemed to be. No matter how down I was, she always lifted my spirits with her bright personality. As she approached me from behind, I was hoping her charm would work its magic again, especially with the way I was feeling.

"Hello Patrick," she said with her usual smile. "I can see you're having one of those exceptionally funky days, aren't you?"

"You better believe it. How do you always manage to pick up on that?"

"First of all, the way you tossed those weights around today was a pretty good indication," she laughed. "Not to mention the fact that you are splashing half the water out of the pool like a big kid."

"You know Jessica, I'm not one to discuss my personal problems, but answer me this. Why are women so fickle?"

She put her hands on her chin as if to seriously contemplate my question, and then responded.

"Probably for the same reason why men are so horny, it's only natural."

I couldn't help but bust out laughing at that one. She had a wonderful sense of humor.

"Well Jessica, thanks to you, I won't have to go to jail for killing my wife tonight," I said sarcastically. "That woman is about to drive me crazy."

"In that case," she said with her hand out. "I'll take my fifty bucks for psycho-therapy right now."

Now that was funny. I had tears rolling down my face from laughter. She really made me feel much better, and boy did I need it. As the announcement came over the PA that the club was about to close, she threw me a towel and asked me to meet her at the front door.

"I have something I want to give you," she said. Without a single dirty thought in my mind, I showered, put on my clothes, and headed for the exit. When I got there she was talking with another female trainer.

"Here Patrick," she said while handing me an invitation. "I'm having a Bulls Basketball Party at my place next weekend. Why don't you and your wife come by and join us? There's going to be plenty of food, and lots and lots of beer!"

"Ok," I said. "I'll see what I can do."

We exchanged casual handshakes and friendly smiles. I put the invitation in my gym bag and walked out the door. As the door swung shut behind me, I could hear the other instructor yelling out. "And don't forget to bring one of your handsome, single friends with you!"

Leaving the club, I felt great. My muscles were tight and my frustration gone, thanks to Jessica. Although she wasn't the most beautiful girl in the world, she definitely had a way of making a man feel like a million dollars. When I returned home, I could see the BMW parked in the driveway. That kind of brought me down a bit because I really wasn't in the mood for another argument. "She's probably waiting at the door with a skillet," I joked to myself. But instead of being greeted by an angry woman, I was overwhelmed by the aroma of food. Nicole was cooking some of her famous Cajun gumbo, and it was smelling good, too. If this was her subtle way of saying, "I'm sorry," I thought, "apology accepted."

As I walked towards the kitchen, I noticed that the table was set with candles and a bottle of wine. "She must really be sorry," I thought. The real shocker was what I saw standing at the stove. Nicole was cooking in a teddy. The one I bought her for our honeymoon. I wanted to jump her bones right then and there, but I waited until after we had dinner. She had gone through a lot of trouble, the least I could do was to enjoy it all. Besides, the food was looking almost as good as she was, and I was starved. After eating half the pot and drinking all of the wine, I carried her upstairs, Don Juan style. I made hot passionate love to her all night long. She didn't even complain about her hair getting messed up. Now, that was really an event.

The next morning we both called in sick. This was the perfect opportunity to turn things around in our relationship. "Who cares about paper work backing up?" I thought. After making love for the second time that morning, we decided to get dressed and go to the movies. While I ran her bath water, she went downstairs to start breakfast. At that point the day was going perfectly, until the phone rang.

"Wait a minute," I thought. "I know for sure that the ringer and answering machine were turned off."

Nicole had obviously switched it back on. I gave her the benefit of the doubt assuming it was either an urgent business matter, or a very brief conversation. What happened next completely and permanently diminished our relationship. She came rushing upstairs as if there was a fire.

"Honey, I'll be right back. Tiffany just had a fight with her boyfriend and she needs someone to talk to."

"You've got to be kidding me. What about our day together?"

"This won't take long. I'll be back by the time you finish breakfast."

Within ten minutes she had washed up, slipped on an outfit, and was out the door. I couldn't believe it. Instead of concerning herself with her own relationship, she chose to run to the rescue of her girlfriend as if she were the neighborhood family therapist. This time the gym wasn't going to be able to ease my pain. Instead I calmly went downstairs, picked up the spatula and finished breakfast. Afterwards, I called in to work and told them I would be coming in that afternoon.

"What's the point of sitting around the house alone?" I figured. "I may as well get some work done."

Before leaving out the door, I remembered to grab my gym bag. I usually went to the health club directly from work. As I cleaned it out, putting in fresh socks and towels, I came across the invitation to Jessica's party. "Boy, I could use some of her good spirits right about now," I thought. For the remainder of the day, I found myself anxiously looking forward to seeing her. I really needed someone to talk to.

At 5:00 sharp, I was out the door and on my way to the gym. This time the pool was my last priority. As I drove into the parking lot, I was hoping to see Jessica's Z-28 parked out front. And sure enough, there it was. I can't remember the last time the sight of an automobile made me feel so elated. I was hoping to catch her at the door to say hello, but she wasn't there. That's when I remembered she was the instructor for the 5:30 p.m. high impact aerobic class. So, I decided to change into my sweats and join in. She was surprised to see me because I usually stayed in the weight room or the pool. As far as I was concerned, aerobics were for sissys and fat people. Boy, was I ever wrong. For the next thirty minutes she took me through a workout more strenuous than Marine boot camp. It was clear to everyone in the class she was trying to kill me. Besides looking in my direction every five seconds, she made sarcastic remarks about my manhood.

"Well girls, do you think these macho men appreciate how hard we work to get into those tight mini skirts?"

Of course, I was the only man in the class at the time. What a coincidence. After the class ended, she sympathetically came over with a towel and a container of water. In a friendly way, I wanted to choke her to death.

"How could you do that to me?" I asked with my hand on my chest.

"I was just trying to make sure all of your frustration was gone from last night," she laughed.

"You did one hell of a job, let me tell you."

"Here, you big baby. Sit back and let me help you relax."

She walked around to my backside and affectionately began massaging my neck, and it felt good. Ordinarily that would have made me very uncomfortable, but I really didn't feel I was doing anything wrong.

"Why don't you take your shower and meet me downstairs?" she said.

"Good idea. I think your workout will last me until next week."

After freshening up and putting on my clothes, I walked towards the front door to meet her. When I got there she was surrounded by a group of men hounding her for her number. As I said, she wasn't a raving beauty, but she had lots of appeal. When she saw me coming she politely told them she had business to attend to. I could see they were pissed off and jealous. But hey, that was their problem. She pulled me into her office and partially closed the door.

"I know this may sound rather forward," she admitted. "But how would you like to join me for a snack and cocktail at my place."

"Well, I think .. ."

"Wait, before you answer," she interrupted. "I want you to know that I understand that you're a married man."

"As I was about to say, Jessica . . ."

"Please allow me to finish," she said as she cut me off again. "It's just that, I never get a chance to talk with you one on one, and I think we could be good friends. Ok, now I'm done."

"Are you sure?" I asked.

"Absolutely!"

"In that case, let's go."

"Are you for real?" she said looking stunned.

"Look," I said. "I'm hungry and I'm thirsty. If your refrigerator is full and you don't have Be Be's kids at home, I'm all for it."

We exited the club as discreetly as possible. People are forever in your business, you know?

I followed her for about twenty minutes to her place.

When we got there she broke out a bowl of spaghetti and some delicious garlic bread. We spent the next two hours on opposite ends of the couch talking about sports and our personal lives. It wasn't long before she got around to asking me about my wife.

"So why doesn't your wife ever join you at the club?"

"She's too busy shopping and getting her nails done."

"Have you ever fooled around on her?"

"Well, aren't we getting personal?"

"I'm sorry," she apologized. "I guess that was going too far."

"No I don't mind, I have nothing to hide. No I haven't even thought about it. Now, let's talk about you. Where is that special man in your life?"

"Nobody wants me," she said as she walked to the kitchen to refresh her drink.

I believe women only say this because it puts the man in a position where he has to tell her how wrong she is. Of course, I took the bait.

"Jessica you are one of the most desirable women I know."

"You really think so Patrick?"

"Sure I do. Any man would be lucky to have you as his woman."

Although she set me up for that response, it was the absolute truth. Physically she was in outstanding shape. No doubt due to the daily workout like the one she put me through. And as for her appearance, she was a little above average. She wore her hair in the popular Toni Braxton style, and she had thick lips like Sade. But most impressively, she was a basketball fanatic. What more could a man ask for? As I said, she had appeal.

That night was the beginning of a wonderful friendship. The following weekend I went to her Bull's basketball party, and had a great time. Needless to say, my wife did not attend. Instead my best friend the plumber, came along. The day after meeting Jessica, he made a very interesting observation. In his exact words, "Man, that woman treats you better than your own wife." And then he said, "You two have a lot in common." That was not the last time someone made this exact same comment. But Jessica and I are only friends. And no! We haven't slept together, yet. Although I must confess, our relationship feels very much like an affair. Is that possible? I say this because she is the first one I call with good news, bad news, and when I need understanding. However, Jessica is not the woman I promised to be faithful to. And until that changes, I'm only going to call my wife when I desire sex. But you must admit, it's a damn shame when another woman has to fill the empty void left by my marriage. Eventually I will have to make a decision about whether Jessica and I can remain just friends. There is no way in the world I can guarantee my feelings won't grow stronger being this close to a woman who treats me so good. I hope my story causes women everywhere to ask themselves one very important question, "Am I my man's best friend?"

One of the most significant reasons why both men and women find themselves in such disappointing relationships is because of the superficial standards they use to determine who will make a good partner. The man, who has watched one too many videos, is looking for a woman with the perfect magazine face and large breasts. While the woman, who has read too many romance novels, is searching for the man with the perfect buns and a large bank account. Not once during courtship does anyone ask, "How do you feel about buying as oppose to renting?" Or, "What percentage of your income do you believe in saving?" And equally as important, "Would you be willing to support me if I wanted to start my own business in the future?" These are questions and issues which need to be addressed before getting married. And most definitely before having children. A gentleman I interviewed from St. Louis also thought he made the ideal choice for a mate. Of course, that was until he told her about his idea to quit his $40,000 a year job and start his own business. Her response was not at all what he expected. She did not kiss him and say, "Oh honey, that's a great idea." Instead, she put her hands on her hips and declared, "Not with my money you won't." All of a sudden her great cooking and physical beauty were irrelevant.

Like so many other women, she failed to realize that her man was not necessarily seeking her financial support. However, he was hoping she would be there to rub his sore back and say, "Hang in there baby, you can make it happen." Or at the very least, offer to lend a hand in her spare time. Obviously, that was asking too much. She turned her back on his dreams, and left him no other choice but to seek support elsewhere. That's right, another woman. She loaned him money, prepared late night meals while he worked, and provided much needed encouragement when no one else believed in him. And today, thanks in large part to her efforts, his business is off the ground and prospering. "So, why doesn't he just leave his wife altogether?" you ask.

Again, you are looking at this situation from the female perspective. As I stated earlier, other factors must be taken into consideration. The most important being his children. He realized a divorce from his wife would result in separation from his two kids, that was unacceptable. And then what about the financial cost. Child support, alimony, and lawyers fees can be pretty expensive. It didn't take him long to do the math and decide the price of leaving was too high. With the business finally making money, and his girlfriend fully accepting his situation, he discovered what so many other wealthy and not so wealthy men have, "It's cheaper to keep her."

The reason why many so-called decent men cheat on their mates often has nothing to do with support or understanding. You know as well as I do, that the number one reason why most men are dissatisfied at home is because of sex. Either they are complaining about the quality they're receiving or the quantity they're being denied. First things first, let's start with the quality issue. No man wants to come home to a woman whom he has to coach into good sex every night. Week after week, year after year, he patiently waits for his wife or girlfriend to elevate her sexual aggressiveness, physical endurance, and fundamental skills. "Ok honey, lift your leg a little higher," he directs. "Don't stop now baby, don't stop." "Ouch, not that way sweetheart!" he shouts.

These frustrating situations take all of the fun and excitement out of sex. And sometimes the level of satisfaction never increases, no matter how hard he tries. As one man put it, "I could tape a cheat sheet on my chest, and my wife would still find a way to mess up." Again, the man has to ask himself that all important question, "Now what will I do?" For the conniving D-O-G the answer would be quite simple, "Get a replacement." For the so-called decent man, this decision takes a bit more studying. After all, he had every intention of living up to his commitment to be monogamous. When he pledged, "To forsake all others," he meant it. However, that was before he discovered her inadequacies in the bedroom. Now all contracts, promises, and bets are off, at least where sexual obligation is concerned. Aside from inexperience and clumsiness, the quality of sex can be affected by the woman's weight, or should I say, excess weight? It's bad enough when you have to play traffic cop in bed, but a crane operator too. Now, that's just not fair.

Some men, however, prefer a full figured woman. And to them I say, "More power to you," literally. You're going to need it. But I think it's safe to say that the majority of men would prefer a woman who was a bit easier to sweep off her feet. Of course, weight is only an issue if someone in the relationship makes it an issue. Nine times out of ten that someone just happens to be the man. Despite the fact he hasn't seen his toes in years, he wants the woman with the perfect body, or near perfect. And God help her if he's seriously into exercising. She'll never hear the end of it. "You need to work on those calves," he'll say. "One hundred sit-ups a night should flatten out that stomach." This is very helpful advice coming from someone who can eat like a pig and never gain a pound. And by the way, when was the last time he gave birth? Men have no idea how difficult it is to lose those unwanted pounds after a pregnancy. Nevertheless, they demand absolute flawlessness. And if they can't get it at home, they'll simply have to order out.

Tony, who is a 25 year old electrician, is one of those men who demands perfection in and out of the bedroom. After being involved in a monogamous relationship for two years, he began seeing another woman to satisfy his sexual needs. When I asked him why he decided to do this, his answer was very critical. "I am not satisfied with my girlfriend's performance in bed. The oral sex is terrible, and she's gaining entirely too much weight." The question many women will surely ask is, "How can he sleep with another woman and still claim to be in love with his girlfriend?" Don't be so ridiculously naive. Love has nothing to do with it. Like most men, he does not equate love with sex. The other woman is nothing more than a temporary sexual bandage to cover the neglectful scars left by his girlfriend. Let's face it, when it comes to sex, women need a reason, while men only need a place. With this in mind, women should stop torturing themselves over the issue of love and sex. It's obvious that men like Tony have decided not to. In his mind there is no conflict of interest. Love is forever, while sex is strictly For Play.

I know people will label me a monster for what I'm about to say, but somebody has to tell it like it is. When I met Tracie, she was 5´ 3″, and weighed 127 pounds. Well, her height obviously hasn't changed, but her weight surely has. As of today she is tipping the scale at a whopping 150 pounds. In my opinion, that is entirely too heavy. And what's so funny is that I met her at a Health Club. She used to work out almost every day. Starting with the stair machine for warm up, then 30 minutes on the treadmill. Sometimes she would come into the weight room to pump a little iron. You name it, she did it. But that was then. Now all she does is sit in front of the television, eat Bon Bons, and watch video taped soap operas. It's like one day she woke up and said to herself, "Now that I've got a man, I can just let myself go." This is so unfair, and women know it. Why doesn't someone come up with a legal contract which requires a woman to stay within ten pounds of her date weight. If she violates this agreement the man has the option of substitution. Sexual substitution to be exact. Doesn't that sound like a great idea? Most women will probably disagree. But I'm willing to bet you most men are sitting around thinking, "Sounds like a winner to me!"

The only reason I even bother going into all of this detail is because I truly love Tracie. She is only twenty–five years old, and I don't want to marry a woman who is going to have a serious weight problem. That's right, I said marry. Because I truly love her and want to get married. But we've got to come to some kind of resolution over this weight issue. And she feels the same way too. Just last month she was talking to me about what areas she needed to work on. "If I could lose about fifteen pounds I would feel better about myself. I've got to lose a few inches from my waist." I couldn't have agreed with her more. But my question is, when is all of this weight reduction and muscle toning going to begin, 2001? I miss the good old days when she was so confident about her figure she would walk around my apartment naked all day long. Now she rushes to turn off the lights, covers up with towels, and dives under the sheets to avoid exposing herself. All that does is draw even more attention to her problem areas. Don't women realize that?

The mental stress of dealing with the weight issue was compounded by Tracie's sexual inexperience. The first few times we had sex were disastrous. She was pulling while I was pushing. When I tried to put her on top, she just sat there as if the bed was going to do all the work. And as for oral sex, forget it! That was a journey into the unknown for her. She was very reluctant to go down on me. I actually had to ease her head down with my hand while she was kissing me on the chest. The more pressure I applied, the more comical her expression became. She would look up at me as if to say, "What in the hell do you think you're doing." I played it off by throwing my head back and moaning, "Awe, that's good baby, right there." Then I put the move on her by angling my body so my penis was right in her face. After I finally managed to get her down there, she spent the next fifteen minutes kissing around it, under it, and on top of it. She did everything except put it in her mouth. That was one of the most frustrating evenings of my life. Two days after that dreadful experience, we sat down and talked about how we could improve our sex life. I promised to be more patient, and she guaranteed me the next time would be better.

Well, one year and two hundred next times later and I still can't get no satisfaction. True enough, she has come a long way in the rhythm department, but she still can't give head. Her main problem is trying not to scrape my penis with her teeth. Sometimes my dick feels like it's been through a shredder. And on those rare occasions when she does manage to do it right, she has the terrible habit of stopping just as it starts to feel good. I hate when she does that. I'm at the point now where I prefer not to have it done at all. Even a hand job every now and then is out of the question with her. She can't even perform that simple task without damaging the equipment. She grips it too tight and bends it from side to side like a damn slinky. After so much frustration, I ask you, "What's a man to do?" Tracie has everything a man could ask for in terms of personality, natural beauty, and loyalty. There's no way in the world I'm going to let another man have her. No way! I will just have to keep working with her to better our sex life. But until then I'll be calling the other woman at 1-900-Do Me Right.

Most women would probably agree that any man who cheats on his woman just because she puts on a few extra pounds, never truly loved her in the first place. However, men do not love as unconditionally as women do. We are visual creatures who live in a society where a great deal of emphasis is put on physical appearance. In our minds, we expect the woman we love to remain beautiful, and thin, throughout eternity. The reality of weight gain is something many of us are unable or unwilling to accept, especially in a new relationship. At the very least we want the opportunity to admire our woman's figure for a few years before the wicked Twinky witch comes along and places a curse on her for life. And if that means Jenny Craig and Woman's Workout World for 40 years, so be it. I will personally flip the bill. But I must say this in the woman's defense; most of this criticism concerning physical fitness, often comes from men who themselves are no specimen of masculinity. They have the nerve to demand absolute perfection while their pot bellies are bulging out of their belts. One man referred to his 42 inch waistline as love handles. The reaction of a woman standing nearby set him straight. "Love handles my ass," she said. "You need to stop drinking all those damned beers and get some exercise yourself."

These unrealistic demands for physical and sexual perfection are the cause of many failed relationships. Most men, including myself, expect women to have it all! Nice figure, attractive face, wonderful sense of humor, well paying job, good parenting skills, master chef, and sex guru. Whew! And if that's not enough, we want the perfect blend of all these qualities. A woman who can win the Ms. Congeniality award by day, and the slut of the year trophy by night. To put it frankly, "We want Halle Barry the Super Mom, and Hazel the Super Freak!" But wait, it gets even more ridiculous! She must then be careful not to be too whorish, otherwise the husband or boyfriend will suspect her of foul play. "Hey baby, where did you learn that move?" he'll inquire. "And when did you start talking dirty in bed?" She's in a no win situation. Either she's too passive or too aggressive. What's a woman to do?

As for the issue of oral sex, let me offer this insightful comment. I haven't met a woman yet who wasn't prepared to go all out to please the man she loved. The question is, however, will he return the favor? Men have a tendency of laying back like porno stars while the woman knocks herself out trying to satisfy him. But immediately after she's done, he's ready to saddle up and start riding. The thought in his mind is, "To hell with you, it's Hammer Time!" This selfish attitude is exactly why so many men have been cut off and left hanging. As one woman remarked, "If I can take the beef, he can go fish."

Men who are successful at getting the most out of their sexual relationships have one thing in common, they ask questions. Instead of complaining and cheating after the fact, they communicate their needs prior to getting deeply involved. Questions regarding acrobatic positions and exotic appetites are not put off until bed time. As one gentleman stated, "Why wait until you're in bed to ask the woman if she feels oral and anal sex are repulsive?" His point is well taken. While men have every right to ask for what they want, the woman likewise has every right to know ahead of time what those desires and expectations will be. As one young lady remarked, "My boyfriend should have told me ahead of time he was into all that freaky stuff. Oral sex is one thing, but booty busting is for prison inmates, not lovers." Another woman was more comical about her experience, "My fiancee tried to pull a Star Trek on me. He tried to boldly go where no man had gone before. So, I sent him where plenty of men had gone before, right out the front door." It is clear these women, like so many others, refuse to submit themselves to the warped expectations of their lovers. And why should they? Not every sex act is natural or necessary to achieve total satisfaction.

One man who has absolutely no complaints about the quality of sex in his bedroom is 37 year old Charles. After five years of marriage, he still feels free to talk dirty, do it in different rooms, and try new positions. Because of this kind of openness in his relationship, he had never been tempted to fool around with another woman. In his words, "My wife Lisa is everything I could ask for in a sex partner. She is aggressive, creative and vocal." However, that was his attitude before his son was born last year. That's when his wife changed from the endless waterfall of passion to the sudden drought of boredom. After spending years working towards the perfect sexual relationship, he now has to contend with his wife's annoying habit of rationing out sex. Even the most decent of men can only endure this kind of torturous treatment before their hormones get the best of them. Charles was no different, he felt perfectly justified in stepping outside of his marriage to seek temporary relief from this frustrating situation. And you know how men spell relief, S E X.

Does anyone have any idea what it feels like to live in a candy store and not be allowed to taste the sweets? Well, I do. Since my son was born a year ago, my sex life has gone down the drain. Instead of doing it five times a week, I'm lucky if I can get some five times a month. At first I thought the problem was physiological, so I didn't press the issue until I thought she was fully recovered from giving birth. But after three months of being patient, I was ready to explode.

"What's the problem, baby?" I asked her. "Is there something wrong that you're not telling me about?"

"I'm just not in the mood," she replied. "Maybe later."

What the hell does, "Not in the mood" mean? I asked myself. She may as well have said, "I just don't want to do it with you," because that's exactly how I felt. As much as I love my wife, I couldn't take much more of her tired excuses. My patience was running thin and my morals were weakening. Matters only got worse when she began breast feeding. I thought I was going to go crazy. For three long months I lustfully watched her, thinking to myself, "Can I have some too, please?"

About five months into this miserable situation, I found myself doing things which were totally out of character. Like staying out late, flirting with strange women, and drinking way too much. My bowling buddies noticed the change immediately because I was no longer rushing home after the game. Of course, they started in on me about my change of lifestyle. And it didn't help one bit that my bowling nick name was Able. You know, like able to come through at crunch time. Well, as you can imagine, they really had fun with that one.

"Isn't it past your bedtime Able?" my teammate Jerry laughed.

"Yeah Able, we know you like to eat while it's hot," Roland added.

"Very funny fellas," I said trying not to sound too pathetic. "Can't we just have a drink without all the wife jokes?"

"What fun would that be?" said Jerry. "Besides, we didn't give you the nickname Able for nothing. Now we might have to take it back since you're not able to get any pussy at home."

They all started cracking up at that joke. And to tell you the truth, I wanted to laugh too, to keep from crying. What I needed was something to keep my mind busy and off of sex. So, before I left the bowling alley that evening, I pulled Roland aside.

"Remember last month when you asked me if I had some spare time to give you a hand down at the cable company?" I asked.

"Yeah, I remember. You turned me down cold. And you know I could use your expertise."

"Well, I'm prepared to take you up on your offer."

"Are you serious, Able?"

"Yes, I'm serious, but only under two conditions."

"Ok, let's hear it."

"One, I only work weekends."

"And two?"

"Two, I want a patch on my uniform top that says Able."

We laughed and shook hands.

"It's a deal. When can you start?"

"This weekend, if at all possible."

"Perfect, I'll see you Saturday morning at 10:00 a.m."

"You better make it 11:00, I might get lucky Friday night."

"Like I said," Roland replied. "I'll see you at 10:00."

When I got home that evening, I told Lisa about the side job. She thought it was a great idea and seemed very relieved. Not only was there going to be a little extra cash to spend, but she knew this would keep me from mauling her on the weekends.

"I think working with Roland is a good idea sweetheart," she said. "At least you'll get an opportunity to utilize some of your electronic skills."

"Yeah right," I thought. She just didn't want me utilizing any of my physical skills around the house, if you know what I mean.

As expected, the job started out pretty boring.

During the first two weeks I didn't do anything except watch the other technicians. On the job training, they called it. "What the hell," I thought. "At least I'm getting paid." Things finally started to pick up after I began working on my own. I was assigned to do the trouble shooting on a new line that was being put in. When that job was complete, I volunteered to do some of the installations for business and residential customers, just to keep busy. That's when the old devil started working on me. Some of the female customers were beginning to ask for me by name when they had a technical problem. Of course, most of their problems were sexual. This went on for six months before I finally got myself in too deep. It was 4:45 p.m. on a Saturday afternoon and I was getting ready to go home when the call came in from a beauty supply distributor. I had installed service there two weeks ago, but the secretary was complaining about a bad connection with her box. Yeah, it sounded interesting to me too. So, I packed my supplies and headed over on my way home. When I arrived at 5:15 p.m., the door was open and the building was empty. I shouted to see if anyone was there.

"Cable man! Is anybody here?"

"Come on in," a woman's voice yelled. "The problem seems to be back here."

When I opened the door to the cafeteria, I understood exactly what she meant by that remark. Regina, who was the secretary, was bent over the television wearing spandex pants with her blouse halfway unbuttoned. I could see the nipples on her breasts without even trying hard. My mouth was wide open, but I couldn't speak. I finally managed to gain my composure.

"So what seems to be the pr-problem," I stuttered.

"Well Mr. Cable man," she said very seductively. I'm having a problem with my reception."

"Let me have a look at it."

As I walked over to the television, I could see that the cable wire had been disconnected in the back. Now I was starting to really get the picture. This was a set up.

"Do you see the problem?" she asked.

"Yeah, I think I have it fixed. Is there anything else you need looked at?"

Why in the world did I have to go and say that. She took advantage of my sarcastic remark.

"As a matter of fact, there's something else I need fixed. Did you bring all of your tools?"

"Excuse me!"

"Don't tell me you don't know what I'm talking about, Able."

"How did you know my name?"

With a seductive look on her face, she walked over to me and pointed at my name tag. We were so close, our lips nearly touched.

"You are Able with the cable, aren't you?" she said while licking her thick lips.

When she said that, I lost all control. Too little sex, and too big a bulge in my pants caused me to hallucinate. Instantly I had become a single, horny, and virile handy man. No wife, no kids, no quilt.

"Miss, I feel it's only fair to warn you," I said while unsnapping my tool belt. "I've been sexually deprived for the last few months, and I'm liable to hurt somebody."

That's when she walked over to her purse and pulled out a pack of condoms.

"Is that a threat or a promise?"

For the next hour I corrected all of her reception problems. First I cleared up all her interference. Then I made sure her box was properly plugged in. By the time I finished, she had received basic and a couple of super stations. All at no additional charge, of course.

Since that day, my marriage has been going much smoother. My wife doesn't feel pressured into having sex, and I don't feel frustrated being turned down. I simply put on my uniform, grab my tool box, and head out for another love connection. And I don't mean for the company either. I'm going to quit that job in a couple of weeks. After all, the whole purpose was to find something to do with my spare time, which I have managed to do. Now I install a different kind of cable. The kind that doesn't require wires or a remote. As a matter of fact, Regina was so impressed with my work, she is considering a hook up at her residence. If my wife is still rationing out sex by the time she calls, I'll be ready, willing and Able to do the job again and again.

Are there any women out there who can sympathize with this unfortunate man? Remember I said sympathize, not agree. Surely there are plenty of men who will not only sympathize with him, but applaud his decision. They know, as I do, that some women ration out sex for the sole purpose of control. It is no secret that women have used sex, or the lack of, to manipulate men into getting what they want. It is nature's erotic tool to hammer out deals and adjust the situation to suit her needs. Likewise, it can be used as a primitive weapon to shoot down a man's ego and kill his masculinity. There is no excuse for playing games with a man's sexuality. Sex is for pleasure and propagation, not for payoff and punishment. For the women out there who have a legitimate physiological or psychological excuse for holding out, my advice to you is, "Seek professional help." Right away! And to those of you who choose to continue using sex as a means to exploit, I say, "What goes around comes around."

CHAPTER 3
THREE TO TANGO

In the game of infidelity there are no innocent players. The other woman is a despicable co-conspirator. The wife or girlfriend is a silent witness to the crime. And of course, the cheating man is guilty as charged. In the end they will all pay for their part in this scandalous lust triangle. Either emotionally, financially, or with the loss of dignity. (Play at your own risk)

VAMP, TRAMP, TRAITOR

If it is true that men who cheat are dogs, then the other woman must be the dog catcher. Because without her full and unconditional cooperation the husbands and boyfriends of the world would have only one place to go, home. Single handedly she can turn a happy home into a house of horror. With little or no shame she will aggressively pursue, wrongfully date, and shamelessly screw any man who tickles her fancy. And she doesn't give a damn if he just happens to be married, engaged, shacking, or seriously involved. As far as she is concerned, the wife or girlfriend is his responsibility, not hers. This type of woman is cold-hearted and careless. She is out for herself and pledges allegiance to no one. Not to her co-workers, not to her best friend, and not even to her own blood. Any man who crosses her path is fair game, no exceptions. As one woman stated, "Women get along just fine at Tupperware parties, business functions, and baby showers. But let an attractive man come into the picture and it's every woman for herself."

It is important to keep in mind that when I talk about the other woman, I'm referring only to those women who are consciously aware of the cheating man's other relationships. The innocent and unsuspecting woman who has been lied to, is not to blame. Unless, of course, she continues to carry on the affair even after she discovers the reality of his situation. Then she too becomes an accessory to the crime. There is no legitimate excuse for any woman to stay with a man once the truth is out. Nevertheless, you and I both know they will still try to justify their dirty deed, either by declaring temporary insanity or blaming the man. For example, one woman said, "By the time I realized he was married, I was already in love with him." Please, give me a break! Women are fully aware when they are dealing with a man who has more than one oar in the water. They simply ignore the obvious signs to temporarily or permanently postpone confrontation. What she should have said was, "By the time I admitted to myself that I was playing the fool, I was already dick whipped." This confession would have been more accurate and honest. Then there is the ever popular excuse of, "All of the nice men I meet are either shacking or married." That may well be true, but that doesn't give you the right to have sex with them, now does it?

For an increasing number of women, the concept of "Man Sharing" is not only tolerable but desirable, or so they say. These are the women I label as Vamps. They consciously and intentionally seek out men who are already involved in other relationships, preferably marriages. And their mentality is crude and unladylike. One woman's statement expressed my point. "When I'm ready to screw, I just pick up the phone and call my fuck buddy," she said. "But after the sex is over, I want his ass out of my house. If he's married, I know he has to go home sooner or later." Women who fall into this category have accepted sex as nothing more than a physiological need and a gratifying sport.

The professional woman of the 90s is a perfect example. She is too busy with high powered meetings and quarterly reports to take time out for a serious relationship. Instead she seeks a man who will not demand much of her valuable time or cause additional stress with his complaining. She has a full agenda, a large bank account, and thin patience. When the man arrives at her condo, she expects him to submit his proposal, execute his business, and promptly leave. There are other clients who have appointments. The older, and more mature woman is also a very good Vamp. She has had enough of fantasizing about Mr. Right. Now all she wants is Mr. Right On Time, with the sex that is. After years of falling in and out of love with insensitive men who only wanted a quickie, she has adopted a new philosophy, "What the hell? I may as well get mine, too."

By far the most interesting Vamp of them all is the cheating married woman. Don't act so surprised, married women are out there creeping, too. Statistics show that 70% of them have cheated on their husbands, at least once. Some would argue the numbers are much higher. Maybe the other 30% were too busy cheating to be surveyed. No matter what the numbers, there is no doubt the married woman is Vamping. And she is often the most adamant about dating married men, only. Not just because they appear to be more stable than the single men who run the streets, but because they can better identify with the inconvenience of her situation. After all, who can better sympathize with a married cheater than another married cheater?

The number of vamps are multiplying every day and there is no sign of a slow down. "What is the cause of this?" you ask. One reason is the over-exaggerated male-shortage statistics. Women are scrambling like chickens with their heads cut off trying to find a good man, or any man with whom they can spend quality time. As one vamp stated, "I just want a piece of the rock, sometimes you have to chisel off another woman's boulder." Again, this is just another weak excuse women use to justify their lack of sexual and emotional control. If only they would take time out to look at the big picture, they could see the problem isn't quantity of men but quality in the man. Until they understand this fact, the cheating man will continue to play them against one another like two pit bulls in a ring and puppets on a string.

And why shouldn't he dog them out? The vamp is constantly setting herself up as an emotional doormat and a sexual outhouse. The cheating man is simply going along with the game and treating her like the whore she is. "If it's sex she wants, then it's sex she'll get," he says. "No love, no affection, and for damn sure, no respect." Millions of men all across this country have adopted this same heartless mentality, and they have no desire or incentive to change. "Why not?" you ask. Because in every night club, office building, and bowling alley in America there is a desperate Vamp willing to spread her legs without a cause or conscience. That's why! And as a result, men have become very cocky towards the women in their lives. For example, a 27 year old gentleman from Chicago told his girlfriend flat out, "If you don't want to get with the program, I'll find somebody who will." And guess what? He had no difficulty whatsoever finding a number of fools who were willing to go along with that so-called program, in less than a week. So much for long term commitment.

Another reason why women are vamping these days is because of the liberal feminist attitude concerning uncommitted sex. I guess this is some form of 60s free love with a 90s condom. The idea is to do it whenever you want, with whomever you want, as long as you use protection. But my question is, "Protection against what?" "Herpes, Syphilis, AIDS?" That's all fine and well, but what about protection against degradation, humiliation, and heartbreak? Even the conniving and calculating Vamp has been known to get burned. Although she may appear to be secure and in control, just wait until she runs into the right man. Or should I say, the wrong man? All of a sudden her busy work schedule and negative past experiences won't make a damn bit of difference. When love calls, she'll pick up on the first ring.

The Vamp usually has very specific taste in men. She prefers a mature man who has his head and finances together, not some young buck she has to make decisions for. Also, she is interested in someone who will always be well groomed and appropriately dressed for whatever the occasion. Close attention is paid to details such as clothes, shoes, brand of cologne, finger nails etc. With the consideration of love aside, she wants the best physical specimen she can get. She also requires a man with a bit of charisma. Someone who can carry on an intelligent conversation without saying y'all, dat, and ain't. But most importantly, her man has to bring his hard hat and lunch box to the bedroom. As one woman said, "What's the point of having an attractive, well dressed, minute man?"

Darren, who is 32 years old and married, says that vamps approach him all the time, especially at the night clubs. His last close encounter took place six months ago with Theresa and Tonya, two Vamps who thought they had everything under control. Well, we'll just have to see about that. As we began to talk about his experience, he shared with me why he thought more women have turned to Vamping. In his words, "Women have become just as low down and dirty as the men whom they criticize." Now, whatever gave him that impression?

When I walked into the club, I could feel the eyes

following me to my seat. As I sat down at the bar, I took inventory of the beautiful women who I might try to talk to, and the perpetrating men who might try to block. While talking to the bartender, I casually glanced around the room to see who was watching. Every now and then I would catch the eye of an attractive older woman who was sitting at the table on the opposite side of the bar. Of course she looked away every time our eyes met. I guess she was checking me out to see if I was expecting company before she resigned herself to coming over. I chilled out and ordered a drink to loosen up a bit. The night was young, and I was in no hurry. About twenty minutes after sitting down and half way through my first drink, the bartender came over to me with a silly looking grin on his face.

"So, would you like another of what you're having?" he asked.

"Slow down bartender, I just finished my first one."

"Well when you're done, the young lady would like to buy you another."

"Hey, that's fine by me!"

Now, keep in mind, he never did specify which young lady it was who offered to pay for my drink. So, I assumed it was the woman who I had been making eyes at. Wrong assumption! When the bartender came over with the drink, I lifted my glass in her direction and whispered, "Thank You." She responded by giving me a flirtatious smile and blowing me a kiss. That gesture obviously set off the woman who actually paid for my drink, because two minutes later I felt a set of large breasts against my back and a soft voice in my ear.

"Are you enjoying your drink?"

"As a matter of fact, I am."

"Well, aren't you going to say thank you?"

"Oh, so you're the generous woman who offered to pay for my drink? Thank you very much."

"I've been trying to make eye contact with you since you walked in," she said. "But I couldn't get you to look in my direction."

"Well, I'll have to pay more attention in the future. By the way, what's your name?"

"My name is Tonya, but my friends call me T N T."

One look at her body and there was no need to ask why. While this conversation was going on, the woman from across the bar was making faces at me. You know that look that says, "Why are you talking to that bitch instead of me?" I wanted to bust out laughing right then and there. I couldn't believe she had the nerve to get jealous. Not after she sat there and tried to play hard to get. "If you snooze you lose," I always say. Tonya turned out to be rather long winded, so I had to cut her off after twenty minutes of non-stop yapping.

"Look baby, I don't mean to be rude," I said while gently holding her hand. "But I'm expecting a few friends. Can we finish this conversation later?"

"Sure, I understand. Just do me a favor and stop by my table before you leave. I'd like for you to meet my girlfriends."

"That's no problem. Where are you sitting?"

She pointed to the tables in the back of the room, handed me her phone number, and strutted away with that vicious body knowing damn well I was watching.

"Thank Goodness," I said to myself. "She was blocking like a motherfucker."

Of course, the story about expecting friends was

only a lie to give the other woman an opportunity to make her move. And I knew she would do just that, after the coast was clear. Oh, by the way, my wedding ring was sitting on my finger as plain as day. Tonya took one look at it then passed me her phone number. She didn't even so much as inquire about my marital status. It was going to be interesting to see how Ms. Cool would react because I had no intentions of taking it off for her benefit either.

Not long after Tonya had gone, I noticed the other woman getting up from her seat. She tried to play it off by walking casually, but I knew where she was headed. I turned my back to make her approach more comfortable. And just as I expected, she was standing behind me at the bar ordering a glass of wine. She was clearly nervous about initiating the conversation. I just sat there eating it up. "Now she knows how uncomfortable it is for us men," I thought. After receiving her change from the bartender, she worked up the courage to tap me on the shoulder.

"Excuse me."

"Well, hello Ms. Cool Breeze," I said as I suddenly turned around.

"Ms. Cool Breeze?" she said with a stunned look on her face. "What did I do to earn that name?"

"Because I was seriously checking you out and you played the cool role on me."

"I wasn't playing cool," she said while making herself more comfortable on the stool next to me. "I was simply being patient. I refuse to act all frantic like these little girls."

"Well, I prefer big girls myself. Would you happen to know one who is available?"

"That depends."

"Depends on what?"

"On how committed you are to your wife," she said while staring at my wedding band.

"Look who's talking. You're the one wearing that Elizabeth Taylor sized rock on your finger."

We both started laughing and slapping five at that one. It was a relief to find that she had a good sense of humor. That's an important quality in a woman, even if you're only bed partners. Which is exactly what this was leading up to.

"Wait a second, we haven't even introduced ourselves. My name is Darren, and you are?"

"Theresa."

"Well Theresa, where do we go from here?"

"To bed, I hope."

"You don't waste any time do you?"

"Darren I am forty two years old. I don't have time for games. Here's my job and car phone number," she said while handing me her business card. "Give me a call Monday afternoon before five o'clock if you're interested in getting together, no strings attached."

She gave me a polite kiss on the cheek and walked back to her table. Within ten minutes, she was out the door. I guess she got what she came for. And to be honest with you, so did I. So, I quickly went over to Tonya's table, met her girlfriends, and said goodbye. Once inside my car, I quickly transferred their numbers into my pocket computer. As I sat there punching in their names, along with their descriptions to remind me of who they were, I shook my head, "These women out here just don't give a damn."

That particular incident took place about six months

ago. And as of today, Tonya is still in my little harem and so is Theresa. But what's interesting about both of these women is how much their attitudes have changed. When I started dating Tonya for example, she told me her first priority was finishing school and starting a business. "You don't have to worry about me bugging you," she said. "I've got business of my own to attend to." Again, that was six months ago. Now this so-called Vamp, who thought she had everything under control, is nagging the shit out of me. My pager goes off at least four times a day because she wants to know when we're going to have sex again. It seems all of her priorities got rearranged after a few rounds with the champ. I'll let her hang around for another month or so, only because she's good in bed. But after that, she's history.

Then there was Mrs. Theresa, oh brother! She turned out to be a real nut case. Our relationship got so intense that she was ready to leave her husband. You should have seen me. I was working harder at trying to keep her relationship together than the marriage counselor and Chaplain put together. The last thing I needed was some over-aged sex maniac chasing me all around town. And what's so funny is that she was the one boasting about turning me out. "You're still young," she said. "I don't want to put a Mo Jo on you." Mo Jo my ass, now look who's walking around all goo goo eyed? She's even got a picture of me in her wallet, which she carries around everywhere she goes. On the back of it she wrote, "This is my man Darren, The Cat Killer." So much for Vamping. When will women ever learn, nobody can be as insensitive and emotionally detached as a man, nobody.

Without a doubt, the most pitiful other woman of them all is the Tramp. Unlike the Vamp who seeks out her victims, she is often chosen by the cheating man because of her willingness to submit to his way of thinking and his way of life. In other words, she is valuable only because she is subordinate and controllable. Women who fit this criteria don't look alike, have the same body shape, or even the same level of education. However, there is one characteristic which is common amongst most of them: low self-esteem. It can be due to physical unattractiveness, economic failure, inability to hold on to a man, or abuse from her past. The cheating man doesn't care one way or the other. He will utilize every advantage available to him to alter the relationship to suit his own needs, sexual needs, to be exact. Remember, this is primarily what the game is all about. The other woman should not fool herself into believing she serves any other purpose except satisfying his insatiable sexual appetite. If you don't believe me, ask yourselves these questions as a test. Do I spend more than 80% of my time with him having sex? And do we spend the other 20% planning when we're going to have sex again? If you answered yes, then you are a tramp. It's that simple.

Seeking out the Tramp has become a semi-annual ritual for 25 year old Rodney. Every six months or so, he sets out to find a new other woman to replace the old one. And he is very specific about what type of characteristics he is looking for. In his own words, "She must be moderately attractive, have big legs, and be able to suck a golf ball through a water hose." Oh yeah, he added one other requirement, "She must be able to make a good pitcher of Kool-Aid." Don't worry, he lost me with that one too. However, I think you get the picture. It will come as no surprise to you that Rodney is cheating on a woman he has been dating for three years. As a matter of fact, he's engaged to be married in six months. I found this rather interesting, so I asked him, "Why would you plan to get married knowing you have no intention of being faithful?" His response was very revealing. "My fiancé is the woman I love, respect, and do nice things for. These other women are only for fun and games. They're like toys I pull down off the shelf when I'm ready to play. And when I'm done, I just put them back until I'm ready again." Listening to this guy really makes you wonder, "What types of women allow him to treat them with so much inconsideration?" My guess would be, the Tramp.

> These women out here are so desperate, they will accept any old excuse for sleeping with you. This is why I find it so difficult to have any respect for them. They are so stupid and accommodating, you can't help taking advantage of them. Janet is the perfect example of what I'm talking about. I met her six months after I started dating my fiancé. Which means May will make three years we've been together. During those three years, I haven't taken her anywhere except to bed. Not to the movies. Not out to dinner. And definitely not out to meet anyone in my family. She has a clear understanding of who she is, and what her responsibilities are, to serve me. Which is the only reason why she is still around. I can call her any time of the day or night and she will come running. As a matter of fact, she was over just last week. I called her from my job at 1:30 a.m. to put in my late night sex order. The conversation was short and to the point.
>
> "Hello baby, this is Rodney. Are you asleep?"
>
> "No, I was just lying here thinking about you."
>
> "Well, I was calling because I need to have you next to me tonight. Can you come over?"

"What time is it?"

"It's about 1:30."

"Ok, give me about twenty minutes or so to get my clothes together for work tomorrow, and I'll be right over."

"Alright baby, I'll see you at around 2:30."

The feeling you get when a woman will get up out of her warm bed to come see you at 1:00 in the morning is exhilarating. You really feel like "The Man." Think about it for a second, this woman was sacrificing precious hours of rest to come over for the sole purpose of having sex. She may have arrived at 2:30, but she didn't get to bed until 4:00. After all, I didn't invite her over to go to sleep. This isn't a government funded shelter, or mission. I invited her over to turn over, on her back.

She never once complained, except the one time I kept her up until sunrise. I'll never forget that morning. Janet woke up late and was trying to rush out to work. I just laid in bed under my warm blanket without a care in the world. I didn't even bother to see her to the door.

"I got what I wanted," I thought. "Besides, she knows the way out."

Completely frustrated and half asleep, I heard her cursing me out under her breath.

"I can't believe this bastard. Here I am running late for work and he can't even get his lazy ass out of bed long enough to make me a cup of coffee or iron my blouse."

But no matter how upset she appeared to be, when I call her again she will get out of her warm bed again to do her duty. Make no mistake about it, she is my personal whore.

Cheryl was another stupid woman who I used to dog out. But she only lasted four months because she refused to accept her position as the other woman. Every week she would complain about not being taken out. In the back of my mind, I knew she wasn't going to last long, especially after our last conversation at my apartment.

"Why don't we ever go out anywhere?" she whined. "I'm tired of lying around your apartment every time we get together."

"Wait one damn minute!" I shouted "Why did you wait until you got over here to start complaining? I'm not stopping you from going anywhere you want to go."

"But I want to go out with you."

"Cheryl, I've told you a thousand times, I cannot be seen all around town with another woman on my arm. You keep forgetting, I have a girlfriend. And I made that clear to you from the very beginning."

"So, I guess I don't get to go anywhere then, huh?"

"Just be patient."

After that pointless conversation, we had sex as usual. But I'm still trying to figure out what in the world I might have done or said to give her the impression she was respectable. She was hired to fill the position of other woman, and that position only. Why she couldn't seem to get that through her thick skull was beyond me. The privilege of being seen with me out in public was reserved exclusively for my fiancé. She was just a piece on the side and had to be kept in the closet where she belonged.

Our relationship came to an abrupt end when she couldn't solve her baby sitting problems. Her sister usually watched the kids on Friday night, and Cheryl would return the favor on Saturdays. But for whatever reason the arrangement hadn't been working out over the last three weekends. One night I got fed up and decided the time was right to get rid of her. I was expecting her at 9:30 p.m., but she didn't call me until 10:00 p.m. with the bad news. That only made the decision even easier.

"Hello Rodney? I don't think I'm going to be able to make it tonight."

"Why not!?"

"My sister faked me out, again."

"Why did you wait this late to call me?"

"As usual, she didn't tell me until the last minute."

"Can't you take them over to your mother's or something? It's not going to take us all night."

"No, not tonight, she's already gone to bed."

"Can't you think of anybody else?"

"Well, I could ask my cousin to watch them, but..."

"But what?"

"But she's gonna want to get paid."

"So, what's the problem?"

"The problem is, I don't have any money. Can you pay her to baby sit tonight?"

"Hell no! I mean, let me get back to you in about fifteen minutes, someone is on the other line."

Needless to say, I didn't call her back, ever. Those damn kids of hers were starting to become a burden anyway. She had ruined my weekend plans for the last time. I was forced to get on the phone and make last minute Booty Calls. Luckily for me, I work well under pressure.

It is obvious the cheating man has no regard for the other woman. She is insignificant and worthless unless her pants are down and her mouth is shut. He could care less about her daughter's kindergarten graduation, her promotion on the job, or even how well her day went. His only concern is whether or not she wants to have sex, period. Any other discussion is nothing more than a waste of valuable time and a nuisance. And don't even think about burdening him with your personal problems. He is the consummate fair weather friend. As long as the sun is shining and everything is going smoothly, he will be calling every weekend with a cordial invitation for fun and games. But let a few minor problems arise in her life, and the cheating man will disappear faster than the last cold beer at a July barbecue. He is there for the good times, not the hard times.

Last but not least, there is the other woman who has absolutely no shame in her game. She is the despicable Traitor. While publicly declaring, "All men are dogs," she is behind closed doors with another woman's man. Often times that man belongs to a close friend or relative. As I mentioned earlier, women get along like ice cream and cake until that attractive man comes on the scene. When that happens, it's a free for all. And the Traitor doesn't care if the girlfriend, sister, or even the mother has made it perfectly clear that she's interested in a particular man first. She is out for herself, in it to win it, and going for what she knows, his zipper. As one Traitor so wisely put it, "It's nothing personal." But what if that man just happens to be a long time boyfriend or husband. In my opinion, that's about as personal as you can get. An example of this scandalous behavior is in the following story. Michelle the Traitor, tells how she stole her best friend's boyfriend from right under her nose. She admits that from the very beginning she had every intention of having him for herself. As she put it, "My friend did not deserve him." Boy, with a friend like her, who needs enemies?

Jo Ann and I met three years ago at the company

where we both work. I was the new trainee and she was my immediate supervisor. Being from out of town, and the youngest of the ladies in the office, I was very nervous my first few weeks. Jo Ann did everything she could to make my transition comfortable. I guess you could say she took me under her wing. Right away we hit it off. To my surprise we had identical taste in clothes, food, and as fate would have it, men. She was a very attractive woman in her mid thirties and I was a tempting 25, what a pair. But our age difference didn't stop us from hanging out together flirting with men. And everything was all fun and games up until last May, that's when Eric entered the picture.

We met him on the same day at an after work party. He was six feet tall, with light brown eyes, and a medium build. And he had buns that made you want to thank his mamma. Yes indeed, he was fine. The odd circumstances surrounding how we all met, made it clear to me that trouble was right around the corner. You see, I met Eric first. He tapped me on the shoulder as I was coming into the club. We exchanged a few words and flirtatious looks before I excused myself to find out where Jo Ann was sitting. In my own womanly way, I left no doubt in his mind that I was interested. But as I walked away, it dawned on me, "I didn't even get his name."

"Oh well," I thought. "I'll definitely run into him later."

Boy, was I ever right about that! After I found Jo Ann, we sat down and gossiped about all the tacky dressed women at work and the horny executives. And of course, I briefly mentioned Eric. We both ordered a glass of wine and talked for a few more minutes before she excused herself to go to the bathroom. Now, this is when things got really interesting.

At least twenty minutes passed, and Jo Ann still had not made it back from the bathroom.

"I hope she didn't get in a fight trying to steal somebody's man," I jokingly said to myself.

But no sooner than that thought crossed my mind, did she show up at the table with you know who on her arm.

"Hell no!" I said under my breath.

I just knew she was bringing him over to me. But this was not the case.

"Michelle, this is Eric. Eric, this is my girl Michelle."

"Hello Michelle, haven't we met somewhere before?" he asked sarcastically.

"I don't think so. Could you excuse me for a second? I need to go to the ladies room."

"Go ahead, take your time." Jo Ann happily replied. "I've got all the company I need right here!"

As I walked towards the restroom, which I really didn't have to use, I began wondering if this was all some kind of sick joke. Ok, so he wasn't my man. And I hadn't described him to her or even told her his name. But you can understand my suspicions, right? Anyway, I checked my attitude and enjoyed the rest of the night. By the time I went back over to the table, Jo Ann was sitting there looking like she had just hit the damn lottery.

"I've got his number, girl. And he's not even married. Can you believe it?"

"Congratulations. I hope you can hold on to this one."

Retrospectively, I realize that my comment was a threat and a challenge. No matter how friendly we were,

I knew I wanted Eric to myself. You can call it competition, revenge, or just spite. To be honest with you, I really don't give a damn.

All the time Jo Ann and Eric were dating, I kept close tabs on how things were going. About six months into their relationship, things started to unravel a bit. I kept my eyes and ears opened, waiting for just the right moment to make my move. And because she trusted me with every intimate detail, my job was all the more simple. Our late night girl talk on the telephone was my best inside scoop. And you know how women like to talk.

"So, how are things going between you and Eric lately?"

"Not so good. We had another argument last night."

"What was it about this time?"

"Can you believe he wanted me to come over to his apartment in a trench coat, with nothing on underneath?"

"No he didn't!" I replied as if to sound disturbed too.

"Yes he did girl. Not only that, but last week he wanted me to give him oral sex in the car while we were on our way to dinner."

"You mean while he was driving?"

"That's right, going 65 mph down the expressway."

"You've got to be kidding me?"

"No, I'm not. But I told him to find him a hoochie if he wanted that type of action. I'm an old fashioned kind of girl."

"Wait a minute, didn't you two have an argument just last week?"

"Awe, that was about my cooking. He complained that my red beans and rice didn't have any flavor."

She would have been better off giving this information to the C I A. Doesn't she know you can't trust any woman with so much insight into your relationship, and especially into your bedroom. I was licking my claws after that revealing bit of news. This was exactly what I had been waiting for, a weak link. Or more to the point, a dissatisfied man. Now it was time to move in for the kill.

The process of breaking them up was going to be a breeze. I had all the details about what he wanted, and more importantly, what she wasn't giving him. And prior to making my final move, I began doing all those subtle things to let Eric know that I was still interested. You know, little things like always taking pictures with him, or playfully sitting on his lap. But my most favorite seductive move was casually putting my hand on his knee whenever we were sitting close together. Jo Ann was so blind and stupid, she didn't even notice. And if she did, she never said anything about it. I wish a woman would put her hand on my man's knee. She would be pulling back a nub.

Anyway, my plan was simple. Talk down about Jo Ann, and pump up his ego at the same time. Men are suckers for that. This way I can blind side him with my proposition without appearing too suspicious. The perfect opportunity came when they had a heated verbal exchange while I was visiting. He stormed out onto the patio, and she decided to make a run to the store to get some air. Another stupid mistake. Now I was alone with him to make my move. I began my subtle attack by sounding compassionate.

"Eric, you've been looking kind of down lately. What's the matter?"

"Oh nothing. You know how your girlfriend can get at times."

"Yeah, she's sweet but she has her moments."

"You can say that again. But she's been having too many of those moments, lately."

"What do you mean by that?"

"Well, that's kinda personal."

"Awe, you can talk to me about it. After all, I am her best friend. And she tells me everything anyway."

"Everything?" he said with a stunned look on his face.

"That's right everything. But don't tell her I told you."

"Did she tell you about the trench coat?"

"Yep, she sure did. And she told me about the request for a nose dive too."

"How embarrassing."

"Don't be embarrassed. I think you are very creative with your sexual ideas."

"I'm glad somebody thinks so. I can't get her to go along with anything that's out of the ordinary."

"Well, I wish I could be of some help."

"Excuse me!"

At that moment Jo Ann walked in with the groceries. But it was too late. I had already planted a seed in the mind and in the crotch of her man. "It will only be a matter of time before his curiosity and his hormones get the best of him," I thought. About a week after that conversation, my prediction came true. He asked me if he could come over to my place to talk about something that was on his mind. But I knew he wanted to do more than talk, and I was right. Without even so much as a hello, we were in each other's arms as soon as the door closed behind him. We both knew what was up. After that day, I began to make myself unavailable to Jo Ann. No more shopping sprees on weekends. No more late night girl talk on the telephone. And no more hanging out at the clubs. That's because the party was now at my place.

As of today, Jo Ann still isn't aware that I am the reason behind Eric leaving her. She still calls me every now and then to talk about how much she misses him. I just sit the phone down while she pours her heart out. A couple of times when she called, Eric was in bed lying right next to me. He loves to start performing while I'm trying to keep my composure. Sometimes he will suck my breast or go down on me while I'm trying to be serious. Here I am going, "Yeah girl, um. I hear what you're saying, ah." I can't believe she hasn't caught on yet. As I said, she's so stupid. However, I must admit, she did teach me something. And that was how to please Eric. By observing her mistakes, I have become everything to him that she wasn't. I've already shown up at his job twice without any clothes under my trench coat. Just last week he almost crashed the car while I was giving him a blow job on the expressway. And as for good cooking, I put Betty Crocker to shame. Chicken and dumplings, fresh baked lasagna, and cakes made from scratch. I'll do anything to keep the man I waited so long and worked so hard to steal.

It's no wonder why the other woman is hated with so much passion. She is selfish, ruthless, and has no conscience. Her philosophy is, "All's fair in lust and war." And her favorite song is, "If that's your boyfriend he wasn't last night." When will she ever wake up and realize the reason why she is the other woman, is because she does not fit the qualifications of a wife or serious girlfriend? Sure, she may be attractive, but only in a sexual kind of way. She may be very supportive, but the wife or girlfriend has seen him through years of hard times. And she may be outstanding in bed, but he knows that a lasting relationship cannot be built solely on good sex. The experience with his mate has demonstrated that. Remember, once upon a time he was probably horny as hell over her too and look what happened.

No, the cheating man is not going anywhere but home. Home to his wife, home to his girlfriend, and home to his children. The other woman should therefore pack her emotional and sexual suitcase and find a man of her own. Otherwise she will be subjected to more unnecessary suffering and pain, especially during the holiday season. Every Valentines Day will bring bitter sweets and broken hearts. Each passing birthday will see her grow older, not wiser. Thanksgiving will have no thankfulness because the chair beside her at the family dinner table will be empty. While Christmas Day will be just another annual nightmare of loneliness and depression. And as for the New Year, it will only remind her of how big a fool she has been the year before. Makes you wonder why they call them Happy Holidays, doesn't it?

PAY TO PLAY

On a typical Friday afternoon, the cheating man prepares himself for yet another weekend of illicit sex. First he contacts the other woman to confirm their plans, then he calls home to tell his usual lie about going out with the boys after work. As the clock strikes 5:00 p.m., everything is set. He signs the office time sheet and rushes out to his car. Once inside, he tunes into his favorite radio station, shifts into drive, and heads for the expressway. But wait, he has one very important stop to make before his secret rendezvous can take place, The Cash Station. When he arrives at the bank, the drive through lines are long and moving slowly. "What the hell," he swears. "I can use this time to figure out how much money I'll need." He reaches for the pen inside his shirt pocket and begins adding up his expenses. "Let's see," he contemplates. "Motel room, cheap bottle of wine, gas money, and a few extra dollars to get me through the weekend." After waiting for what seemed like hours, he finally makes it to the front of the line. He punches in his PIN number and decides to withdraw $60.00. Now he's ready to bump and grind.

This scenario replays itself millions of times every weekend all across this nation. Men are emptying their wallets, charging up credit cards, and bouncing checks, all in the name of lust. And although the dollar amounts may vary, the cheating man will inevitably pay for his horny impulses, and pay dearly. Whether it's for a sleazy motel room, a tank of gasoline to get across town, or ten bucks to help pay for his lover's baby sitter, the dollars quickly add up. The attitude of one man regarding this unnecessary sexual overhead was simple-minded and unemotional. "It's all in fun," he boasted. Well, if this is true, why doesn't he just go down to the local comedy club for laughs? That way he could avoid spending all of his hard earned money, and eliminate the risk of contracting a potentially fatal venereal disease. However, the unfaithful men of the 90s are uninterested in such a logical alternative. They prefer to perpetually submit themselves to a lifestyle which is self-destructive, morally wrong and economically costly. When will they ever learn that money cannot buy love, happiness, or fulfillment? Judging by the jam packed motel parking lots on Friday night, the answer seems to be, never.

The cheating man has earned the reputation as the cheapest man on earth. Though he may be blessed with good looks, an impressive wardrobe, and proficient sexual skills, he is often one paycheck away from being on the streets. In other words, all of his assets are on his ass. Of course, you would never know this by the way he swaggers around the club as if he owned a Ferrari, and lived in the most posh area of town. Chances are, he got a ride to the party with a friend and lives at home with his mother. However, being cheap has nothing to do with income or net worth. It is more a matter of generosity. For example, if a man who earns a million dollar salary is only willing to spend $1,000 per year on his mistress, he would be considered a tight wad. On the other hand, if a bus driver earning $30,000 per year were to spend that kind of money on his lover, he would likely be perceived as very unselfish. As I said, it's not about how much a man rakes in, but how much he's willing to dish out.

Which brings us to the cold monetary reality of the cheating game. Most men who have relationships on the side don't want to spend one thin dime. Their number one priority is to get the best sexual bargain on the market. If they had to choose between a beautiful mistress who insisted on going out every weekend and a moderately attractive woman who didn't complain about staying indoors and having sex, guess which one they would choose? That's right, the low maintenance, low budget ugly duckling. But even the most unattractive lover can be a financial burden around the holidays. Therefore, the miser cheating man will intentionally shy away from any serious relationships between December 25 and February 14. And if he's already involved, then he will quickly and creatively find a way to get uninvolved.

The plan is simple, instigate a fight with the other woman just before the holiday arrives. This argument can be over bad sex, phony jealousy, or flaky dandruff. What difference does it make? The objective is to keep as much money in his pocket as humanly possible. And if he's really a cheapskate, he will come up with some sort of unorthodox religious restriction. "I'm a Muslim baby," he'll declare. "We don't recognize these commercialized, European holidays." Yeah right. Just last month he was drinking beer, smoking cigarettes, and stuffing his face with chitterlings. As for birthdays, well, the cheapskate cheating man has a plan to avoid celebrating that one too. Out of no where, he will come up with a close relative, old army buddy, or make believe offspring who's birthday just happens to fall on the same day. What a coincidence.

This financial game of bargain basement sex will eventually catch up with the corrupt, and insensitive, cheater. Although he may have been successful at avoiding the direct cost of infidelity, such as lavish dinner dates and luxurious gifts, he will soon discover there are indirect costs which can be even more expensive. One man who can testify to the truth of that statement is 32 year old Anthony. During the two years of his affair, he has gotten away with not taking his mistress out anywhere except to Burger King and White Castle.

"I got her where I want her," he boasts. "The lovin' is good, her body is tight, and the price is right. What more could a man ask for in a skeezzer?" Of course, this was his attitude before last month's eye opening experience. That's when he discovered what so many other horny fools have before him. Sooner or later, you've got to pay the piper.

Have you ever had one of those days that felt like God was trying to tell you something? Well, I have. And it came on a cold rainy Friday in January. It began innocently enough with a sick call to my job. I complained to my supervisor about having stomach problems, but in reality I was simply too damned lazy to get out of bed. After putting on an outstanding performance, I layed back down and tried to go back to sleep. But for some strange reason I couldn't relax. Amazing, isn't it? One minute you're tired as hell, and five minutes after you decided you're not going to work, you feel like the Energizer bunny rabbit. It must be psychological.

I decided to take my new found energy and put it to good use at the gym, which happens to be located in the basement of my building. I sprang out of bed, ate a light breakfast, and put on my sweats. As usual, the place was empty. "Don't these stupid people know they're paying big bucks for these amenities," I thought. After working out for about an hour or so, I went back upstairs and took a cold shower. By 10:30 a.m., I was bored as hell. I felt like a kid ditching school with nothing to do. That's when I got a page from Angela, my mistress. I could see by the number on the pager that she was calling me from home. "Why isn't she at work today?" I wondered. As I picked up the phone to return her call, I thought about how long it had been since I was able to call another woman from the privacy and comfort of my own home. What memories. After allowing her phone to ring three times, I figured she must have accidentally put in the wrong number. She had a bad habit of doing that. Just as I was about to hang up and try her at work, she picked up.

"Hello," she gasped.

"Hello to you Ms. Hooky Player. And what may I ask, are you doing at home?"

"I took one of my vacation days. I didn't feel like putting up with those ignorant ass customers today."

"So, what took you so long to pick up the phone?"

"I was just about to get into the shower when the phone rang. The cordless was downstairs in the living room."

"Well, since you worked so hard to get to the phone, I'll let you in on a little secret."

"Don't tell me, you took off of work today, too?"

"How did you know?"

"First of all, you never return my phone calls so soon. And secondly, the weather outside is shitty."

"Very good Ms. Sherlock Holmes. Now tell me what's up."

"Well, I just wanted to hear your voice, but since you're off from work, I'd like to find something for you to do."

"Something to do like what?"

"Like coming over here and getting on your JOB, that's what. A woman doesn't live by bread alone, you know."

"Tell you what baby. Let me throw on a pair of jeans and grab my garment bag and I'll be right over to punch in," I laughed. "How's noon?"

"Perfect!" she shouted. "You'll be just in time to <u>be</u> lunch. And let me warn you sweetheart, I'm starving. See you at 12:00. Bye."

Angela was the ideal mistress. She was moderately

attractive, childless, and most importantly, affordable. Never once in two years had she ask me to take her out or buy expensive gifts. All she wanted was a little conversation and a lot of TLC, both of which I could easily afford.

However, getting over to enjoy this economical date presented a transportation problem. My wife had driven the Honda Civic to work that day and our other car, a 1992 Corvette, was stored away in the garage. We both agreed not to drive it until Spring or unless there was an emergency. But on that day, I would break my own rules. The weather outside was terrible, and the only emergency was my hard dick. I thought about waiting for my wife to get home with the Honda, but the idea of answering questions didn't sit too well with me. So, being the typical horny male, you know it didn't take long to make a decision. I put on my blue jeans, threw a business suit in my garment bag, and grabbed the car keys off the hook. Before leaving, I wrote a short letter lying about attending an important business engagement across town. Then I wisely called my secretary and asked her to cover for me if my wife was to call. After putting all the safeguards in place, I strolled out the door ready for a high impact, low budget workout with Angela.

So there I was, driving in the pouring rain during the lunch time rush. The traffic was bumper to bumper and people were driving like lunatics. To make matters even worse, there was road construction going on, three lanes were merged into one. It must have taken me 20 minutes just to get down the expressway ramp. But once I got beyond the construction area, it was smooth sailing. For the next 10 miles traffic was light and moving at a constant 55 mph. That is, until I arrived at the tollway where traffic was backed up again. "Why don't you stupid people have your change ready when you get up to the gate," I angrily shouted. After another 20 minutes of pulling my hair out, I finally got through the toll and made it to Angela's place. "What a trip!"

Looking at the clock in my car, it was 1:00 p.m. I was an hour late. Having wasted enough valuable time, I quickly grabbed my cellular phone and garment bag, put The Club on the steering wheel, and turned on the alarm system. Don't get me wrong, it's not that Angela lives in the ghetto, but the neighborhood isn't exactly Mayberry either. Anyway, when I made it up the front steps, Angela was waiting with the door open. As usual, she was half naked and smelling like the perfume department at Marshall Fields. After putting down my car phone and hanging up my garment bag in the closet, we went straight upstairs to the bedroom. It took me all of 5 seconds to tear off my clothes and get between the sheets. However, I did slow down long enough to put on my condom. Forgetting to do that would be a definite no no.

By 3:00 p.m., we were both exhausted. My mouth was completely dried out and Angela's stomach was growling like crazy. We put on our robes and went downstairs to make something to eat. She put a couple of steaks in the oven, and I shredded a head of lettuce for a salad. At 5:00 p.m. the food was ready. While we sat across the table from one another she made all kinds of obscene gestures with her food, licking the steak and rolling her tongue around the fork. It was clear she wanted more sex, but I was tired and my tank was empty. After cleaning our plates, she quickly put away the dishes and guided me back upstairs to screw my brains out, again. But before she could make her move, I begged for mercy.

"Please baby, I'm only human for God's sake."

"Awe, come on Tony," she said while stroking my chest. "I know you have a few more rounds in you."

"Food always makes me tired Angela, especially when it's raining outside. Just let me relax for a minute."

"Remind me not to feed your ass until after round two next time."

"Very funny. Now stop hogging the blanket and let me get some rest."

I told her to set the alarm clock for 7:00 p.m., which would have given me enough time to put on my business attire and make it home by 8:00 p.m. The day had gone perfectly, up to that point. The sex was great, the food was good, and the bed was warm. "All of this pleasure and relaxation for the price of a tank of gas," I thought. "What a bargain!" But my monetary celebration was premature. As I fell into a deep sleep, the price of passion was about to multiply.

It was 11:15 p.m. when I was awakened by the sound of my car alarm. I leaped out of bed and lifted up the foggy window to see two young kids going through the inside of my car.

"Get the hell away from there!" I shouted.

One of them gave me the finger while the other grabbed what he could carry, and off they ran around the corner. Angela turned on the lights and handed me my pants. I just looked at her and shook my head. She had intentionally neglected to set the alarm clock. This was just another one of her silly attempts at trying to cause trouble. I wanted to smack the shit out of her, but there was no time for dramatics. So, without saying a single word, I ran downstairs, grabbed my car phone, and slammed the door behind me. After turning off the alarm, I inspected the inside of the car to see what damage had been done. The passenger's side window was completely busted out, and the seat was soaked with rain. Everything inside was gone. CD's, insurance papers, telephone stand, everything. "Thank God they weren't professionals," I thought. "Otherwise I would be walking home." I cleaned the glass off the seat, covered it with plastic, and headed for the expressway. I was totally disgusted. My so-called cheap date had already cost me an estimated $600.00. But the night was still young.

When I arrived at the entrance ramp to the expressway, I looked over at the digital clock inside the car, it read 11:30 p.m. "My ass is definitely in for it tonight," I said to myself. "How am I going to explain being out this late without calling?" The frustration and anxiety of the situation only made matters worse. There I was 40 miles away from home with no CD's, no window, and no excuse. As I drove down the desolate expressway, my foot turned into a block of cement. The speedometer read 75 mph. That was way too fast to be driving on wet pavement, but I didn't care. I had to get home and every minute counted. The chilly night air was blowing freely through the broken window, but I was so pissed, I didn't feel a thing. I was determined to make it home before midnight. And just as it looked as if I was going to make it, guess what happens. That's right, I get pulled over by a State Trooper for speeding. "God, please don't let this be some cowboy who's had a bad day," I prayed. But that was asking for too much. As he approached my car, I let the window down, and reached inside my jacket to get my license out.

"Keep your hands where I can see'm boy!" he shouted.

"Oh shit, it's John Wayne!" I said under my breath.

"Don't move until I tell ya to."

"What's the problem officer?"

"The problem is, I've got a report of a stolen Red Corvette, and you are speeding like this is the damn Indianapolis 500."

"Well, if you will allow me to get my license out, I can prove the car is registered to me."

"Why don't you just do that."

I slowly pulled out my wallet out and handed him my license. I didn't want the situation to turn into Rodney King part II.

"Stay right there son, I'll be right back," he said with an annoying southern accent.

He walked back to his car and punched up my license on his computer. Within five minutes he was on his way back. But this time his attitude was less hostile and more professional.

"Look Sir, I'm sorry about the harsh language but sometimes you never know."

"No problem officer."

"However, I will have to give you a ticket for driving 70 mph in a 55 mph zone. And since the roads are wet, I'll also have to cite you for driving too fast for conditions."

"Look officer, Can you give me a break? I've had a terrible day: I'm late getting home and my car has been broken into."

"Well, looks like your day is about to get even worse."

He handed me two tickets, and had the nerve to tell me to have a nice day. "Yeah right," I thought. I put the car in drive and pulled out into traffic. At that very moment, I swear I wanted to cry. "Why do all the worst things seem to happen to me, when I am out somewhere I have no business being?" I contemplated. But I already knew the answer to that question.

After that experience, I never saw Angela again. I didn't even bother going back for my clothes. I simply tacked it on to the price of the lesson. As for my wife, she didn't say a single word to me that night. The look on my face was so damned pitiful she decided to have mercy. The next morning I went to the dealer for an estimate on the damage. The cost was $699.20. However, after adding on the $100.00 for the traffic tickets, and the .80 for the tolls, it came out to an even $800.00. Let this be a lesson to cheating men everywhere, it really isn't worth it.

The cheating man's inability to control his hormones will eventually catch up with him. One day he will make the mistake of not using protection, and the result will be 18 to 21 years of child support. Now he will pay to play whether he likes it or not, either by choice, or with a little motivation from the court system. Men who find themselves in this predicament act as if they are totally stunned by the choice of their mistress to go through with the pregnancy. "How can this bitch do this to me?" he swears. "We didn't even have a serious relationship." Well, maybe it wasn't serious to him, but for her it was as serious as a heart attack. The underlying problem seems to be the man's blatant ignorance and total disregard for the feelings of his lover. Just like any other woman, she is an emotional creature who equates love with sex. Her vagina is not merely an outlet for his animalistic desire, but an ultra sensitive nerve connected to her heart. So, while he's on top of her moaning and groaning, thinking it's all in fun, she is slowly but surely falling in love. Now she won't be so easy to get rid of. After years of climbing in and out of his bed, the mistress also feels she has made an investment. An investment which she has every intention of collecting on. And if that means having his baby, then so be it.

This kind of mentality is typical of women who are desperately lonely and have very low self esteem. Rather than finding a man who is willing to consent to fathering their child, they prefer to set a sex trap and trick him into it. This is by far the most disgraceful and stupid thing a woman could ever do. But no one is more stupid than the cheating man for allowing it to happen. He is the one who has everything to lose. His family, his peace of mind, and his money.

One year ago, Anthony and Carey, who are both 27 years old, learned exactly how expensive cheating can be. However, it was Carey who learned his lesson the hard way. Either by accident or design his mistress Stephanie came up pregnant only two months after they started having sex. His world was forever changed and his wallet forever lightened. According to the laws in his state, she could be entitled to as much as 20-30% of his salary. Which amounts to nearly $350.00 to $400.00 a month. What a price to pay for a few nights of meaningless sex. Anthony, who is single with no kids, could only empathize with his partner and learn from his mistake. Hopefully there's a lesson in it for other cheating men out there.

> This nightmarish ordeal began in August when Carey and I met Stephanie at the mall. A mutual friend who managed one of the clothing stores introduced us. She had a very nice personality, but her body was not

quite up to my standards. On a scale from one to ten, she was about a six. Her breasts were too small and she didn't have much ass either. But what she did have was a flirtatious smile and a vacant bed. As it turned out, that was all she needed to attract Carey's attention. From the very beginning, I warned him to be very careful with her. Although she appeared to be a nice person, her credentials were shaky. No college, no career, and as far as I was concerned, no future. I'm always leery of women who fit into this category because they have absolutely nothing to lose.

Like most women who are trying to trap a man, Stephanie made herself available 24 hours a day. Carey could call her anytime of the day or night and she would drop whatever she was doing to do him. On at least two occasions, he called her at 2:00 a.m. to have sex. And just as I expected, she was more than willing to get out of her warm bed to let him in. Now, that may sound appealing to some men, but it taught me one valuable lesson. Dealing with a woman who has too much time on her hands can be extremely dangerous. Anyway, after about two months of dropping by for late night quickies, he became bored with her and broke off the relationship. From that point on, her name was never mentioned again. Not until three months later when she called him with the shocking news of her pregnancy. Of course he called me immediately after he hung up the phone with her.

"Tony, this is Carey, do you have company?"

"No I'm alone, what's up?"

"Man, I hope you're sitting down for this one."

"Stop tripin' and spit it out."

"Do you remember that female we met at the mall

about four months ago?"

"Which one?"

"The one I used to call and wake up at 2:00 in the morning. You know, the plain Jane."

"Yeah, I remember her vaguely. So what about her?"

"Well, she just called me a minute ago and told me she was pregnant!"

"Hell naw. You've got to be kidding me."

"I wish I was. I'm getting ready to go over to her place right now and talk to her about getting an abortion."

"Wait a minute, weren't you wearing a condom?" The phone got quiet for what seemed like hours. I knew then what the answer was going to be.

"As a matter of fact, I didn't use one on a couple of occasions."

"Oh shit. You messed up big time."

"I'm not even sweating it. I'll just go over there and threaten to kill the bitch if she doesn't get rid of it."

"Listen to me carefully on this one Carey. Don't even waste your time with that approach. This woman is not going to have an abortion, trust me."

"How can you say that when you don't even know her?"

"First of all, you haven't slept with her since early October, right?"

"Right."

"Now here it is late January, and she's just now calling to tell you that she's pregnant. Come on man, what does that tell you?"

"I'm fucked!"

Later on that evening, he called me with the update on what happened with their visit. Just as I expected, she refused to get an abortion. She lied to him and said she didn't know she was pregnant until her fourth month. Not only that, but she claimed her doctor advised her against an abortion because of medical reasons. Was that a bunch of bull or what?

As the months passed and the delivery date grew nearer, Carey became more frustrated and hostile. The thought of a stranger having his baby was eating him up inside. This was definitely not the type of woman he wanted to bear his child. "Why me?" he would angrily shout. "I should go over there and throw her ass down a flight of stairs." Although this remark was meant only as a joke, it was clear he didn't want her to carry the baby to term. During this time, he cut off all communication with her. The way he saw it, there was nothing for them to discuss until after the baby was born. And besides, he didn't want to give her the impression he was supporting what she did. In his mind she was nothing more than a conniving bitch who took advantage of him, and that's exactly what she was.

On the day the baby was born, Carey was calm, cool, and collected. I guess he was simply glad it was over. He even went down to the hospital to see the baby, it was a boy. But I strongly advised him against signing any papers until after having a blood test. Sometimes you never know. There are women out here who will get pregnant by a bum, and say it's yours just to save face with their families. A man should always double check to make sure that a child belongs to him. I don't give a damn how long you've known a woman or how much they tell you the baby looks like you.

When he returned from the hospital, his concerns shifted from what he was going to do about the baby, to how he was going to break the news to his wife.

"Tony, how am I going to look my wife in the eye and tell her I have a son by another woman?"

"Well, if I were you, I would just wait for the results of the blood test before I start running off to confession."

"You might be right."

"I know I'm right. I mean, why break the news to her when you're not absolutely positive yourself?"

"You've got a point there, I'll wait."

Two weeks after the baby was out of the hospital, he called her and demanded to have a blood test before signing the birth certificate. She had the nerve to get upset, and threaten to take him to court. When he called me back, he didn't know what to do. I simply told him to stand by his demand, "Tell that bitch you don't know her from Adam," I said. "She can't expect you to trust her when you don't hardly know her last name." Apparently the idea of going through expensive lawyers and time consuming court procedures made her more reasonable. The blood test was taken, and another wait had begun.

"I hope this test comes back inconclusive," Carey said. "I would never mess around again."

"You need to stop that damn lying."

"Ok, then let me say, I will never have sex without protection again."

"I'll let that one slide, for now."

"I'm serious, Tony. This is the most stress I've ever been under in my entire life."

"You've been stressed out? What about me? I've had to listen to your whining for the last ten months. Hell, I feel like I'm the one having the baby."

"Speaking of listening to my whining, I want to thank you for being there for me. You kept me from making even more stupid mistakes."

"Hey, that's what friends are for. Now take your sentimental ass to sleep and let me get back to my company."

"So, you've got another victim over, huh?"

"Yes I do have a date over. And you better believe I've got condoms, jells, diaphragms, birth control pills, and IUD's workin' over here. I'm not taking any chances. Thanks to you, I've become a contraceptive Guru.

Within five weeks, the results of the test came back. But unfortunately for Carey, it was 99.9% in favor of his being the father. Just as promised, he signed the birth certificate and put his son on his health insurance. After only a few nights of meaningless sex, it now seemed that Stephanie got everything she wanted. A beautiful baby, a handsome father, and $350.00 a month. And while he despised her for what she did, he only had himself to blame. After all, he was the one who had everything to lose, not her. He should have done a better job at protecting his own interest. Now he has to face his wife with the painful truth. And God only knows how she's going to take it, especially since she's been bugging him for years about having a child of their own. His excuse was always the same, "We can't afford it." Well, after this expensive mistake, he may be right after all.

Any man who has had the unfortunate experience of having an unwanted child will tell you it is one the most aggravating and powerless feelings in all the world. First of all, the woman has all of the rights and options. She can either get an abortion, put the baby up for adoption, or leave the man out of the child's life altogether. But what rights or options does the man have? To screw or not to screw, that's what. Because after he puts his little wee wee inside of her body, all of his powers are instantly transferred. Now his financial fate is in the hands, or should I say, the uterus of his lover.

Then there are the ferocious fights over paternity and child support. "It's not mine," the man will swear. "I don't know how many other men you've slept with besides me." For the mistress who has been totally faithful, this is a slap in the face and an embarrassment. She knows the baby is his and demands that he support it. "If you don't want to help me out voluntarily, I'll just have to take you to court." Now the situation gets blown all out of proportion and everybody suffers. The mistress will have to secure a lawyer and take days off from work to attend court proceedings. And after all of this wasted time and money, the cheating man will end up paying retroactive child support anyway, so what's the point? It seems to me their energies and financial resources would be better spent on the innocent child, not shifty lawyers.

The cheating man's compulsive desire to have more than one woman is not only monetarily costly but potentially dangerous. It won't be long before his web of deceit snares a woman who's venom is more poisonous than his own, and whose mind is as unstable as a rocking chair with one leg, She will be his worst nightmare come true, a real life Fatal Attraction. In the beginning of the affair, she will appear to be a sweet, rational, and sane individual. But when he tries to dump her, LOOK OUT! She will not react passively by crying herself to sleep listening to Nina Simone albums. Instead she will become savagely enraged and seek revenge on the one person whom she feels is responsible for causing her so much misery. And guess who that is?

Robert, who is 35 years old, discovered first hand just how ferocious one of these women can be. For three long months, his ex lover stalked him all over town. She followed him home, to the gym, and even to the park where he took his daughter to play. "She seemed so docile and harmless when I met her," he said. "What in the world could cause a woman to change so dramatically?" Chances are she was crazy long before he ever met her. All she needed was a little pressure to make her snap. And snap she did.

Kelly and I met at a fundraiser for underprivileged children back in June. I noticed her the minute she walked into the room because she was wearing a sharp pants suit and eye glasses. It's something about business attire that turns me on. As fate would have it, our tables were directly across from one another. When we made eye contact, I greeted her with a hand gesture and took my seat as the speaker came to the podium. Since her back was to the stage, she had to turn her chair completely around to see him. And every now and then she would casually glance over her shoulder to see if I was looking. And of course I was.

After the opening presentations, people began to walk around and mingle, including the three couples who were seated at her table. I expected Kelly to do the same, but she just sat there sipping on her glass of water. That's when I decided to make my move. As I pulled my chair back from the table, she smiled as if to say, "Come and get it." I approached her with my hand extended.

"Hello, my name is Robert," I said as we shook hands. "How are you doing this evening?"

"I'm doing just fine Robert. My name is Kelly. Nice to meet you."

"I guess it was pretty obvious that I was coming over, huh?"

"Well, at the risk of sounding conceited, yes it was. But I must admit, you were rather smooth about it."

"Thank you for noticing. So, what brings you out to such a worthy cause?"

"I love helping children."

"Yeah, so do I. As a matter of fact, I have one of my own."

"Boy or girl?"

"A three–year–old girl. Her name is Tamera."

"Awe, and I bet she's cute too."

"Of course, I think so," I said proudly.

After going through this corny routine of getting comfortable with one another for about fifteen minutes, I decided not to waste any more time dilly dallying around. It was time for the big question.

"So, are you married, engaged, or in love?" I boldly asked.

"None of the above," she responded with a smile. "But what about you? I know some woman has her claws in you already. And it's probably your baby's mother."

"Well, I'm not going to lie to you. We still see one another, but it's nothing serious."

"Yeah, right. That's what they all say."

"Look, I'm not going to waste time lying to you about my situation. If I'm interested in getting to know someone, I tell them my status up front. That eliminates all of the unrealistic expectations and game playing."

"I don't know about you Robert. You seem like a real bad boy. And sooner or later, bad boys have to be punished."

"What in the hell does that mean?" I thought to myself. "Is she into sadomasochism? Or is she merely joking about my aggressive behavior?" At the time, it really didn't matter. All I wanted was those seven digits.

"So what are you trying to say? You don't trust me?"

"Let me share something with you Robert. I've only been in town for two months, and already I've heard that line about a thousand times."

"Oh really, where are you from?"

"Connecticut."

"Connecticut?" I said with a curious look on my face. "You mean to tell me there are black folks in Connecticut?"

"Very funny," she laughed. "Yes, we have blacks in Connecticut. Not nearly as many as are here in Chicago, but we do exist."

"Let me stop cracking on your hometown and get back to the point. I want to see you again. Can't we work something out?"

"I'll tell you what," she said. "Let me have your number, and I'll think about it."

"Think about it!?"

"That's right, I said think about it. An innocent 26 year old woman like myself has to consider what she's getting herself into. And so should you for that matter."

"There goes another one of those odd remarks again," I thought. "Is this woman trying to tell me something or what?" When I think back on it, she was probably trying to warn me. But my mind was tuned into only one thing, getting her out of that wool suit and under my satin sheets. I wrote my home number down on the back of my business card and handed it to her. As the guests began to return from the lobby area, I charmingly kissed her hand, and went back to my table. It was up to her to take it from there.

It was Saturday afternoon when I gave up on hearing

from Kelly. I figured six days was plenty of time for a woman to call me, if she was interested. Later that evening, I thought about calling my girlfriend Donna to ask her out to party, but I remembered she had plans to take my daughter to a birthday party. There was no way in the world she was going to be rested enough to go out after dealing with those wild kids all day. So, I called my best friend Allen instead. He is a party animal and is always game to hit the town. As the phone rang, I was sure he would be screening his calls. And just as I expected, the answering machine picked up.

"Hello this is Allen. Sorry I'm unavailable to answer your call. At the tone leave a brief message and I'll see if I can fit you into my busy schedule." (Beep)

"Busy my ass," I laughed. "You haven't had a date in months."

"Look who's talkin'," he said as he picked up the phone ready to signify. "If it weren't for Donna, I don't think you would ever get any."

"Is that right? Well, at least I didn't get handcuffed to a bathroom sink by two stick up women."

I was referring to an incident which happened a year ago when Allen was robbed by two women at a motel. He was lured to a motel room by a woman he met at the club who promised him a night he would never forget. And she was right, her girlfriend was waiting with a gun. They took his wallet, jewelry, and even his eyeglasses. Allen always had on expensive eye wear. After robbing him blind, they made him take off all his clothes, pose nude for several minutes, and then handcuffed his wrist to the bathroom sink. It wasn't until 11:30 the next morning that the cleaning lady found him buck naked, sleeping on the floor. How embarrassing. But little did I know, he would soon get the last laugh.

"Now why did you have to go there," he laughed. "How was I supposed to know they wanted to play cops and robbers instead of doctor and nurse?"

"Let me stop dogging you partner," I apologized. "I called to ask if you wanted to go out to our favorite spot tonight?"

"You know I'm game. What time do you want to meet up?"

"How about 10:00 p.m? That way we can get our usual table."

At that moment, someone was trying to call me on my other line.

"Is that your line or mine?" Allen asked.

"It's mine, hold on for a second." (Click)

"Hello?"

"Hello, may I speak to Robert?" a woman's voice requested.

"This is Robert. Who's calling?"

"Oh, you've forgotten me already, huh?"

"Look, I don't mean to be rude, but I don't like playing guessing games."

"This is Kelly, remember me?"

"Well, hello stranger! It's about time you called. I thought you faked me out."

"No, that wasn't it at all. I just wanted to think about what I was getting myself into. Have you thought about it?"

"What's there to think about? We're two consenting adults, right?"

"If you say so."

"Kelly, I'm on the other line with my friend Allen right now. We're thinking about going out tonight.

Would you like to join us?"

"Sure, why not?"

"Would you like for me to pick you up?"

"No thanks, I'll just meet you there."

I gave her directions to the club and the time we would be there. I then clicked back over to Allen and told him about my unexpected date. He was anxious to see if she measured up to my physical standards. But I was more interested in whether or not she measured up to my sexual standards. She was cute, but I needed a freakazoid.

When I arrived at the club Allen was already there with a woman under his arm. He introduced us and ordered a round of drinks. I rested my jacket on the back of the chair and began looking around for Kelly.

"So where is your date Romeo," Allen joked.

"She said she would try to be here by 10:30 p.m. but you know how long it takes these women to get dressed. First they have to pile on a ton of war paint. Then they'll spend an hour trying to squeeze into a dress that's two sizes too small."

"Yeah, but you men love it, don't you?" His date said with her hands on her hips.

"You damn right we do!" Allen and I both replied.

"That's what I thought."

"So, what's Kelly wearing?" Allen asked.

"If I know her, she'll probably have on a pin striped business suit. She seems very conservative."

By 11:00 I hadn't seen anyone who fit Kelly's description. Once again I thought she had faked me out. I walked around looking for her until a woman asked me to dance. "What the hell," I thought. "No sense in spoiling a perfectly good evening." We danced for about twenty minutes before I noticed this fine woman on the far end of the floor, getting busy. "If I didn't know any better, I'd say that was Kelly," I thought to myself. "But there's no way she would be wearing that black cat suit." After looking harder, I could see that it was her after all.

"Excuse me," I said to my dance partner. I need a break."

"Maybe I'll see you later, she said with a flirtatious grin."

"Yeah. maybe."

I quickly ushered her off the floor and headed for the area where Kelly was dancing. And there she was shaking and grinding to the music. Damn she was looking good! I finally got her attention by waving my handkerchief in the air. She immediately broke off her dance and came to me.

"Where have you been all night?" she said sounding exhausted. "I've been looking all over for you."

"Yeah right. And I guess you expected to find me behind the guy you were dancing with?"

"Well I did, didn't I?"

"I guess you've got a point there."

"So where is your friend Allen?" she asked.

"He's at the table, you want to meet him?"

"Sure, but let me freshen up a bit first."

"You look fine, let's go."

She wrapped her arm around mine and I escorted her over to the table proud as a peacock. When we got there, Allen and his date were hugged up like two teenagers.

"Excuse me love birds," I interrupted. "I'd like for you to meet Kelly."

"Hello, pleased to meet you," Allen's date said.

"Wait a minute!" Allen shouted. "This is Ms. Connecticut? No wonder they kicked you out the state. With an outfit on like that you're probably illegal."

Kelly reacted by laughing and slapping him five, which kinda shocked me. She seemed so laid back and country when we met. Now she was a sociable, seductive, dance machine. But I liked it, I liked it a lot. For the next couple of hours we talked, drank and told stale jokes. When the party was over, I invited her over to my place for a night cap. This turned out to be a big mistake. I was about to disclose my residence to an absolute psychopath. But once again, my smaller head was making all of the decisions.

It was 2:00 a.m. when we made it upstairs to my apartment. After hanging up our jackets, I offered her something to eat. But she wasn't hungry, at least not for food.

"Do you have a towel I can wash up with?" she said.

"Sure I do," I replied while reaching into the linen closet. "Use this one."

"What about a t-shirt?"

"Ah, no problem, is there anything else I can get for you?"

"I'm not making you uncomfortable, am I Robert?"

"Absolutely not," I lied.

I could feel the sweat pouring down my back and the bulge growing in my slacks. She casually grabbed the towel out of my hand and went into the bathroom. As the door closed behind her, I went into action. First I took my pants off and put on a pair of shorts. Then I turned on 95.5 WNUA to set the mood. I love listening to jazz when I'm having sex. Finally, I took a couple of condoms out of my drawer and put them in my pocket, just in case. Shortly after setting my trap, I heard Kelly calling for me to give her a hand.

"Robert!" she shouted. "Could you come here for a minute?"

"What is it?" I asked from outside of the bathroom door.

"I need you to hand me the soap."

"No problem!"

The bathroom was foggy and hot. I grabbed the bar soap out of the soap dish, and I reached my hand inside the shower curtain hoping to catch a peek.

"Here you go," I said as her hand took the soap. All of a sudden she pulled my arm and the rest of my body into the hot shower.

"Hey! What are you doing?"

"Just relax and enjoy the sights," she said.

In a very exotic fashion, she reached down and unsnapped my shorts. I tried to speed up the process by giving her a hand, but she wouldn't let me.

"I'm doing this," she protested.

"Be my guest."

For the next thirty minutes we had passionate sex underneath the shower head. Luckily for me I had my soggy condoms on hand. We did it standing up, on our knees, and against the wall. She was so flexible I could have bent her over the curtain rod. "This is too good to be true," I thought to myself. When the morning came, I found out just how right I was.

When I woke up the next morning, Kelly was staring down at me with those spooky light brown eyes. I couldn't tell if she was admiring my body or regretting what had happened. Without saying a word, she sprung off the bed and into the bathroom. Figuring she was ready to go, I put on my robe and opened the blinds. It was a beautiful Sunday afternoon. Just as I was about to go make breakfast, Kelly came back into the bedroom ready for more.

"Where do you think you're going, mister?" she asked.

"Well, I was going to the make breakfast."

"Never mind that. I want to nibble on you for awhile."

After reaching inside my headboard cabinet for another condom, we were at it again. But this time she was talking crazy while we were doing it.

"Oh Robert, you're so fine. Give it to me baby, come on. Deeper, deeper."

"You want it all baby?"

"Yes, all of it, from now on. You're my man now. You're mine."

"Chill out with that kind of language Kelly. I don't respond well to possession."

"Don't ruin the mood Robert, I'm just talking."

I let her statement slide and went back to getting busy. She was a complete wild woman, growling and screaming, "Fuck me, fuck me!" After an hour of this unappealing session, I got up and went to the bathroom. That's when the telephone rang and the answering machine picked up. It was my girlfriend Donna.

"Hi honey it's me. I just called to remind you to meet us at the park at 2:00. Tamera has been asking about you all morning, so don't be late. Oh yeah, how did it go last night at the club? I know Allen was acting a fool as usual. Sorry I couldn't make it. Anyway, I'll see you at 2:00, bye."

From inside the bathroom, I could hear Kelly mumbling under her breath. When I walked into the living room she was rushing to put on her clothes.

"Hey, what's the rush?" I asked.

"I can't believe you Robert."

"What are you talking about?"

"I guess I was the back up date for last night, huh?"

"Look, all I did was ask you out. What's wrong with that?"

"Nothing except that you lied to me about the status of your relationship with your baby's mother. You two have something serious going on. I may be young, but I'm not stupid."

"How in the hell can you gather all that by listening to a phone call? All she did was remind me to come see my daughter. I do that every Sunday afternoon."

"I don't want to talk about it right now, I'm a little upset," she said as she grabbed her purse and headed for the door.

"Wait a second," I shouted. "I don't even have your number."

She stopped momentarily to write down her pager number. I convinced her to give me a minute to put on my shorts so I could walk her downstairs. After I escorted her to the lobby, I dashed back to my apartment and threw on a pair of old blue jeans to meet Donna and Tamera at the park. As it turned out, that would be the last time I enjoyed myself at the park without looking over my shoulder.

For the next three days, I was out of town on business. I called home every night to check my messages, but Kelly hadn't called. Thank God. She was getting too intense for me. When I got back in town on Wednesday afternoon, I stopped by the apartment, dropped off my bags, and went to the office for a short conference. By

4:00 p.m., all of the meetings were wrapped up and I had received time off for a job well done. All I had to do was meet a client downtown at 7:00, have him sign some papers, and the next five days were mine. When I went to my office to collect my things, my pager was beeping like crazy. Within thirty minutes, I had received three calls, which was very unusual for me. "Who in the world could this be?" I wondered. I dialed my voice mail and pressed in my code to retrieve my messages.

"Hello Robert, this is Kelly. Why haven't you called me?" I really need to talk to you. Call me back right away. (Beep)

"In case you didn't get my first message, this is Kelly again. I need you to call me back immediately, this is urgent!" (Beep)

"Look Robert, I don't know what kind of game you're playing but you're fucking with the wrong woman. Either call me back this instant, or I'll come see you. And you won't like it!" (Beep)

"What is this woman's problem?" I asked myself. I dialed the number she left me on the pager twice, but no answer. When I called my answering machine at home, there were three identical messages on it. She was seriously tripin'. But I didn't have time to deal with her at that moment. I had an important meeting downtown and I needed a quick shower and a nap. I collected all of the contracts, threw them into my briefcase, and headed for home.

When I drove up to my apartment building Kelly was parked out front in her red Hyundai. I parked my Saab in the underground lot and went to see what she wanted. As I approached her car, she jumped out with her hands on her hips, she was pissed and ready to explode. But instead of making a scene outside in front of all those people, I insisted that we go upstairs to my apartment. She locked her doors, grabbed her purse, and followed me to the elevator. I lived on the 25th floor, so the conversation began immediately after the last person got off on the 5th floor.

"What is your problem leaving me those kinds of messages?" I shouted. "Are you out of your mind?"

"What else was I supposed to do?" she whined. "You didn't call me for three days, or return my messages."

"That doesn't give you the right to call me up talkin' crazy. And it damn sure doesn't give you the right to stake out my apartment like a detective."

As the elevator doors opened onto my floor, we held our tongues until we got past the nosy neighbors who were in the hallway. Once inside my apartment, I sat her down on the sofa, and played back her messages on the machine. Can you believe she had the nerve to start crying?

"I'm sorry Robert. I didn't mean to say those nasty things. I just wanted to talk to you, that's all."

"Get up, and come with me!" I shouted.

I walked her into my bedroom and pointed at the unpacked suitcase lying on the bed.

"I've been out of town on business for the last three days. I can't just drop everything I'm doing to call you, understand?"

"I said I was sorry," she sighed. "What else do you want me to say?"

"Right now I'd like for you to say goodbye and leave."

"But I don't want to go," she said as she put her arms around my waist. "Let me make it up to you."

"I don't think that's possible Kelly."

"I'll do anything you say Robert," she said as she began to unsnap my pants. "Just don't ask me to leave."

All of a sudden my complaining stopped. She pulled down my slacks, dropped to her knees, and began giving me oral sex. And while I was standing there moaning and groaning trying to keep from biting my lip off, she somehow managed to undress herself and maneuver me onto the bed. I couldn't believe it. There I was having unprotected sex with this deranged lunatic after she had threatened me over the phone and come over to my house unannounced. "What am I doing?" I asked myself. But once again, my horny flesh took over my common sense.

The next time I looked up at the clock on the headboard it read 6:50 p.m. I had to hurry to make my appointment.

"Kelly, get up!" I shouted.

"What's wrong baby?"

"I have somewhere to go."

"I'll just wait here for you."

"That's not a good idea. I want you to leave with me."

"Come on Robert, I'm comfortable. How long are you going to be anyway?"

"Look here, I'm not going to go through interrogation when I'm ready to leave my own house. Now get up and put your clothes on."

That did it. From that point on I would see the real Kelly. She quickly slipped on her sun dress and strapped on her sandles. While I ironed my shirt, she started mumbling under her breath and giving me the evil eye. I had a feeling she was about to snap, and I was right.

"I bet you let Donna's ass stay here when you're gone."

"What did you say?"

"You heard what I said you no good bastard. I bet Donna doesn't get kicked out after she's been fucked."

"That's it!" I shouted. "Get your crazy ass out of here before I throw you out."

"Don't worry, I'm leaving. But remember what I told you in the beginning, you should've thought about what you were getting yourself into. You're not going to treat me like some kind of street whore and get away with it."

"Just get the hell out of here!"

She gave me the finger and slammed the door so hard one of my paintings fell off the wall. "Now I've done it," I thought. "After all these years of fooling around, I've finally run into a real life fatal attraction." I had already seen the movie three times, and knew Kelly definitely had Glenn Close potential. I didn't want to admit it, but I was scared. From that day forward, the hunter became the hunted.

For the next three months, Kelly made my life a living hell. She would call at all hours of the night, leaving crazy messages about getting even and teaching me a lesson. She even threatened to cut off my penis like Lorena Bobbit did her husband. Ouch! After a month of these disturbing and frustrating calls, I had my number changed. But somehow she managed to get the new one. I figured either she, or someone she knew had caller I.D. Now I had to pay an additional cost to the phone company to have a block installed, and for another new number. This is where the dollar amounts and the mental duress really started to add up.

After the phone calls stopped, the stalking began. Every weekend she would park outside of my apartment and sit there as if she was at a drive-in movie. I was tempted to send down a box of popcorn and milk duds but I didn't want to provoke her. The last thing I wanted to do was let her know she was getting to me. I simply ignored her and went about business as usual. That was easier said then done. When I pulled out of the underground parking, she began to tail me all over town. She followed me to the grocery store, to the gym, and to church. But she finally crossed the line when she showed up at the park one Sunday afternoon while I was visiting with my daughter.

Donna had to be told about what was going on. There was no way of knowing how far Kelly would go. But somehow, I had to come up with a convincing story to explain why this crazy woman was stalking me. Telling her the complete truth was not even an option. I decided to drop the news late one Sunday evening after visiting with Tamera. As her phone rang, I took a deep breath and prepared to go into my act.

"Hey sweetheart, how are you doing tonight?" I politely asked trying to soften her up.

"Fine baby, what's wrong? Did you forget something when you dropped off Tamera?"

"No, that's not it. This involves another woman."

"I'm listening," she said sounding worried.

"First of all, where is Tamera?"

"She's asleep. What's with all the mystery?"

"Ok, remember last year when that guy from your job kept calling you and sending you flowers?"

"Yeah, what about him?"

"Well, I have a woman who's fixated on me."

"So that's why you've changed your phone number twice in two weeks. I knew something was going on. How serious it is?"

"Very serious I think. She followed me to the park today while I was with Tamera."

The phone all of a sudden got silent. I could hear what sounded like footsteps and then a door squeaking shut. I'm sure she went to make sure Tamera was asleep and that her bedroom door was closed before she went off.

"If that bitch comes near my baby, I'll kill her! I mean it."

"Calm down Donna."

"Calm down my ass. What's going on Robert? Are you telling me everything?"

"Look, this woman was just a client who wanted to mix business with pleasure. When I turned her down she became obsessive, that's it."

"I'm going to trust you on this one Robert. But don't let me find out you're lying or it's over between us, I'm serious! Now tell me what this crazy woman looks like so I can watch out for her."

I told her everything I knew about Kelly. How she looked, how she talked, and what type of car she drove. All I could do was hope this whole thing would end before the stakes got too high. I had already lost my peace of mind, I wasn't about to lose the only woman I ever loved as well. But Kelly was a very sick young woman who was bent on revenge. She felt rejected and disrespected. How does the biblical saying go, "Hell hath no fury as a woman scorned." Well, I was about to find out first hand just how true a scripture that was.

Three weeks had passed since the incident in the

park and it seemed that Kelly had finally retired from guard duty outside of my apartment. I was so relieved, I decided to take Allen and Donna out to our favorite spot for drinks. I told Donna we were celebrating a successful business deal, but in actuality I was just happy to drive out of my building without seeing that damn red Hyundai parked across the street. Allen and I met inside the club at 10:00 p.m. We grabbed our usual table and ordered beers while we waited for Donna to arrive.

"So where's Donna?" Allen asked.

"She had problems finding a babysitter, but she's definitely coming."

"How is she handling all of this drama?"

"So far everything has been going pretty well, especially since Kelly stopped tripin'."

At that moment the waitress came over with our beers. I thought it would be the ideal time to propose a toast. I lifted my bottle and stood up from my stool.

"To Kelly, may she find another man to terrorize, or move her crazy ass back to Connecticut."

"Amen," Allen toasted.

For the next half hour we sat there sipping on Miller drafts and checking out the beautiful women coming in. Of course all I did was look, but Allen was foaming at the mouth. I had to remind him that Donna was very tight with one of his girlfriends. He checked himself and ordered another round. Shortly after we finished our second beer, the waitress came over with another drink on her tray.

"Excuse me," she said politely as she sat the drink down in front of me. "This drink is from a secret admirer."

"What is it?" I asked.

"It's a Bloody Mary."

"Where is the woman who paid for this drink?" I urgently asked.

"Right over there," she replied while pointing in the direction of the bar.

When I looked over I couldn't see anyone who resembled Kelly. But I knew for a fact she was the one who pulled this sick joke.

"What did she look like?" I demanded.

"She was kinda short, with a petite build. And she had light brown eyes. Can I get you anything else sir? I have to get back to work."

"No, thank you," I said.

As the waitress walked away, I could see Donna making her way over to the table. She was looking good, too. Her hair was freshly cut, and the dress she had on was hugging every curve. For a 32 year old woman, she's got a great figure. I tried to remain cool, but I had a feeling something was about to go down. I wasn't going to hang around long enough to find out if I was right. So when Donna walked up to the table, Allen and I immediately started making excuses to leave.

"You're looking good tonight baby," I complimented. "Let's go get something to eat instead of sitting around here."

"Good idea," Allen agreed. "I'm starving."

"That's fine by me," Donna said. "But let me have one drink before we go."

I quickly flagged down the waitress hoping to order the drink and get the hell out of there as fast as possible. While Donna sipped slowly on her strawberry daiquiri, Allen and I practically stood guard until she finished. And just as we were about to leave, guess who shows up? That's right, Kelly. She stood directly in front of the table with a bottle in one hand, and the other behind her back. She was sloppy drunk and looking spooky as ever.

"Hello Robert," she said. "Aren't you going to introduce us?"

"I don't think so," I said as I positioned myself in front of Donna.

"Well, the least you could do is thank me for the drink I sent you."

"Look Kelly, I don't have time for your childish games."

"Kelly!?" Donna shouted. "Are you the sick bitch that's been following my child into the park?"

"No, I'm the sick bitch who's been following your man into the park. I have no interest in your nappy head child."

"So what is it that you want, heifer?" Donna asked.

"I want to teach your old man a lesson about toying with a young woman's emotions. He's not going to dip his little stick in this fountain of youth without paying for it."

"Woman you are out of your mind," Allen said.

"You shut up four eyes and mind your own business!" Kelly screamed.

That's when she lifted the bottle over her shoulder and hurled it in our direction. Everybody ducked. After the bottle smashed against the floor, I looked up to see Allen's bloodied face. She hit him directly in the eye, which caused his glasses to cut through his skin. The swelling began immediately.

"You crazy bitch!" I shouted. "Look what you did."

"You should be more concerned about what I'm going to do to you."

In one motion she swung her arm from around her back and began violently throwing what looked and felt like large steel darts. I quickly pulled Donna down onto the floor and shielded her with my body. I felt two sharp objects pierce my back side. One in the upper back and the other in my buttocks. Once she was out of ammunition, Donna jumped up and ran towards her like a mad woman. Kelly tried to run but Donna grabbed her by the hair and slung her to the floor. By this time, the music had stopped and all eyes were focused on the cat fight. Even the bouncers stood by and watched.

"I'll kill you bitch, I'll kill you," Donna threatened as she ripped Kelly's blouse off and smashed her face against the floor.

"Let me up," Kelly begged.

"Not until I knock some sense into your young ass."

I ran over to where the fight was taking place with the two darts still inside me. I started to break it up, but Donna was giving it to her good. So, I stood by like everybody else and watched. After a few more scratches on the back and punches in the face, Donna let her up and the security guards moved in. We were all escorted to the back office where the owner was waiting. Allen and I knew him personally so the police were not called. Kelly boldly admitted to starting the whole thing and offered to pay for the damages. I chose not to press charges since Donna kicked her butt and nobody was seriously injured. Allen, on the other hand, got even by slapping her in the face as she was escorted out of the club. But unfortunately this wasn't the end of it. When I got to my car, the tires had been sliced and the windshield was completely smashed out. On the hood there was a message carved in the paint that read, "Now we're even motherfucker."

The most fatal attraction of them all, is not the woman with a weapon in her hand, but a disease within her body. While the cheating man swears up and down his hot blooded lover is clean and healthy, she could be burning with herpes, syphilis, or even AIDS. And just as he neglected to wear a condom to prevent pregnancy, he will likely neglect to protect himself from contracting a lethal disease. It is a well known fact that many men carelessly and foolishly stop using contraception after they've become comfortable with their lovers. That's a hell of a decision considering whose life is at stake. His own and the life of the innocent wife or girlfriend who is dumb enough to continue to trust him.

This is why the cheating men of the world must take time out and ask themselves, "Is it worth it? Will I continue to dishonor myself and threaten my family's mental and physical health? Or will I take charge of my relationship and stop engaging in such a risky and dangerous lifestyle?" These are very important questions for any man who is a man. Because it is only a matter of time before the high cost of infidelity hits his wallet, hits his conscience, and hits home. When this happens, he will lose his most valuable asset of all, the woman who truly loves him. And she won't be as easily replaced as money. Nor will her anger and loss of respect be as easily remedied as with a shot of penicillin.

WAKE UP!

Why do so many women get involved with men whom they suspect are cheaters? And more significantly, why do they remain in these relationships even after their suspicions have been confirmed? The answer to that question would of course depend on which woman you ask. Some romantically claim, "It's because of love." While others openly admit, "It's all about the money." But these so-called reasons are nothing more than lame excuses for the timid wife or girlfriend to hide behind. In my opinion there can be only one common denominator for such universal tolerance, and that is fear. More precisely, the woman's fear of being alone.

This paralyzing dread of waking up to an empty bed, and growing old without a mate is all the leverage the cheating man will need to take complete control and full advantage of his relationship. He has predetermined there will be no serious repercussions for his actions. The men I interviewed for this book are the perfect examples. They bragged openly and arrogantly about their methods of cheating with no regard for who might read it. And although names have been changed to protect the guilty, there was an air of absolute certainty that the games would continue in spite of what was revealed. As one gentleman boldly stated, "It doesn't matter what I tell you about how I cheat. Once a woman falls in love with me, she's not going to listen to anyone telling her anything. She won't even listen to herself." He is clearly depicting women as too stifled by emotion to act on any obvious proof of infidelity, and he's not alone. Several other men promised to purchase a copy of this book to give to their wives and girlfriends as gifts. What audacity!

It is because of these condescending attitudes that women must stop allowing themselves to be degraded and humiliated by the men who so emphatically claim to love them most. They should slow down, back up, and reevaluate what a true relationship is all about. Otherwise the lying, cheating, and dogging out will go on forever. What it boils down to is four simple questions. Questions which the love struck woman must look in the mirror and ask herself. "Do I know my man is cheating? Do I really want to know? Will I act on the obvious signs? Or am I truly blinded by love?" For the cheating man, the entire process of fooling around seems to be viewed as an elaborate game of chess. For you, the female reader, it should be considered as a very serious wake up call.

Teaching women not to condone infidelity in their relationships is not a simple task, especially if they were raised in an environment where it was perceived as normal behavior. Karen, who is 28 years old, can relate very well to this type of subservient upbringing. At a very young age she was brainwashed by her mother, aunts, and other female family members into believing, "Boys will be boys," or as I stated earlier, "Dogs will be dogs." For years she accepted this foolish philosophy as gospel and quietly went along with the program. But after years of being neglected and disrespected, she finally woke up and smelled the coffee.

> My education about men cheating began at age fifteen. That's when I first started to notice my father was staying out late and going away for weekends, supposedly with his buddies. My mother never once complained, she just went about raising my brother and me, as if nothing was wrong. But sometimes I could see the frustration come out. She did a great job of disguising it by fussing at him about leaving his empty beer bottles on the living room table or playing the music too loud in the basement. This was her only way of getting back

at him, at least as far as she was concerned.

My mother was a very attractive and intelligent woman. She had a bachelors degree in English and a body that would have given a 25 year old a run for the money. That's why I never understood why she put up with my father's cheating for all those years. His ongoing affairs were clearly annoying her but she never threatened to leave him. I'll never forget what she used to tell me when we were alone, "Marriage is forever baby, no matter what." By the time I was seventeen, she began to preach about a few other things as well. Things that had a dramatic impact on the way I would view my own relationships.

A family wouldn't be complete without a gossiping aunt or a know it all friend of the family, I had both. My Aunt Dorothy, and my mother's girlfriend Carolyn were a hell of a duo. Every Sunday afternoon they would come by the house while my mother cooked dinner. Of course, this was the signal for my father and brother to escape to the basement, and my cue to get lost. However, on one particular visit no one asked me to leave. It was obvious by the way they were all grinning that my indoctrination into the girls club was at hand, but my young mind was ill-prepared for their bold and eye-opening conversation. As expected, loud mouth Aunt Dorothy started in on me about my new boyfriend Jason.

"So I hear you've got a man, Karen," she said as everybody all of a sudden got quiet.

"Dag, why are you all in my business Aunty?" "Momma I told you not to tell her."

"Girl, your momma can't keep a secret," Carolyn laughed. "If you want something broadcast to Europe, just tell your mother and watch the ten o'clock news the next day."

"Carolyn you'd better be glad my daughter is in here," my mother responded. "Otherwise I would tell you to kiss my ass."

"Let's not get off the subject," Aunt Dorothy said. "Tell us about him."

I wanted to run out of the kitchen, but being allowed to hang out with the girls was too much to give up. And besides, you know how young girls like to boast about their boyfriend. So I leaned back against the counter, poked out what little chest I had and started bragging.

"Well, since you insist," I said. "Let me give you the scoop. He is a freshman in college, his family owns their own business, and he's fine as wine."

"Oh my goodness, you'd better put a chastity belt on her Joanne!" Carolyn shouted. "Her panties are on fire."

"Yeah sis, I think you need a drink," Dorothy said while comically pouring my mother a glass of water. "Puberty has finally kicked in."

My mother just looked at me and smiled. She knew I wasn't a loose young woman. And her and my father trusted Jason not to pressure me. But shortly after the jokes stopped, the education began.

"So what are you going to do when he starts fooling around on you?" Carolyn asked.

"Get rid of his butt," I declared.

"Is that right? And then what?"

"And then I'll find a man who's not going to cheat on me."

They all busted out laughing. My mother spilled her water and Carolyn damn near fell out of her chair. Aunt

Dorothy walked over to me, and sympathetically put her hands on my shoulder. "Baby, ain't no such thing as a man who won't cheat."

"Amen to that," my mother added.

At that moment, the phone rang, it was Jason. After excusing myself from all the playful teasing, I went into my room to talk. We had plans to get together later that evening, but he said he couldn't make it. As usual, I didn't complain. But I must admit that the idea of him cheating on me did enter my mind. It was clear that a seed had been planted in my head about trusting men, or should I say, *not* trusting them.

Growing up watching my older brother David cheat on his girlfriends also had an effect on my attitude about tolerating infidelity in my relationship. He and his friend Chris would talk about women as if they were play things. And since I saw them as fairly decent men, I figured whatever they had to say was representative of most men, including Jason. One day, not long after Aunt Dorothy's lecture, I dipped in on a conversation they were having on the porch. Needless to say, I was more attentive then ever.

"So what's up with that young lady you met at the club a couple of weeks ago?" Chris asked.

"You mean Debbie?"

"Yeah, what ever happened to her?"

"She's still around, but I don't think she's going to work out."

"Why is that?"

"Well, for one thing, she asked too many questions about my girlfriend. And secondly, she's not giving it up!"

That really made me mad. They had some damn nerve dissing that poor girl just because she wouldn't have sex. And if she would have fucked him on the first date they would have called her a slut. "Why are men like that?" I angrily contemplated. What really bothered me, however, was the thought that Jason might possibly start feeling the same way about my holding out. "How long do I have before he dumps me for some whorish college student?" I wondered. For the moment I put those thoughts aside and continued to take notes.

"What about that little filly you met at the skating rink?" my brother asked.

"Oh, you're talking about Rhonda," Chris said sounding cocky. "She's on her J-O-B."

"You mean she's in your B-E-D," my brother laughed as they slapped five.

"Yeah, she could definitely be a keeper, if only she would stop coming over while she's on her period."

"Man, don't you just hate that?"

"That's alright though, I've figured out when her time of the month is. I'll just put off our dates until I know it's over. Which reminds me, I need to run to the store."

"For what?"

"Well, I already have a little black book for phone numbers, now I need a little red one for menstrual cycles," he joked.

Those words cut through me like a hot knife through butter. "Was Jason avoiding me for the same reasons?" I wondered. There was only one way to be sure. I tiptoed away from back door and ran upstairs to check my calender. Like most young women, I kept track of every event from our first kiss to our last argument. If there was any relationship between canceled dates and my menstrual cycle, I would find it. And sure enough, there it was in black and white. He called me the day before my period to cancel our dates for the last three months. My heart dropped, and my eyes watered. "I can't believe Jason played me like this," I cried. This was the turning point in my attitude towards men. I had completely bought into the "All men are dogs" theory. The way I saw it there was only one thing left for me to do, secure mine.

Within three months, I was popping birth control pills like Tic Tacs and having sex. I was determined to hold on to Jason at all costs, which I did long enough to get married to him. I was 21 years old in my third year of college, and he was 23 and about to graduate. What a fairy tale relationship right, wrong!

Three years of matrimony and two beautiful children later, and Jason was still up to his same old tricks of putting me off to see other women. He was real smooth with it too. Not once in seven years did I ever find any physical evidence of his cheating, but there were plenty of other signs that he was out creepin'. On Saturday afternoons for example, he always refused to take the kids with him when he claimed to only be going shopping. Then there were the Masonic meetings which lasted for five hours on Friday night. When I went over to my mother's house to express how I felt, she went into her usual speech about keeping the family together at all cost.

"Mom, I don't know if I can handle much more of Jason's game playing."

"What exactly do you mean sweetheart?"

"Come on Mom, you know what I mean, his affairs. And I mean affairs with a capital S."

"Look baby, I know Jason isn't perfect, but he is a good man. Doesn't he provide well for his son and daughter?"

"Yes."

"Doesn't he manage the household money well?"

"Yes."

"And doesn't he come in at a decent hour?"

"Yes momma, but."

"But nothing child," she said as she stopped cooking and came to sit down at the table. "You've got to learn that a man is going to be a man. And as long as he's giving you your respect, you've got to leave him alone and concentrate on keeping the family together."

"Giving me my respect!" I shouted. Every time he leaves the house to see one of his whores he's disrespecting me. Why should it make any difference because I don't have fingerprints or video tape. I know damn well when my husband is cheating."

"Keep your voice down Karen," she said while gesturing with her hands. "Your father is right downstairs."

"Good, maybe he'll get the hint and stop messing around on you."

Smack! In one motion she leaned across the table and slapped me dead in the mouth.

"You watch your mouth when you talk to me young lady, I'm still your mother!" she shouted. "Don't you worry about my business with your father. We've managed to stay together for 26 years and put two kids through college. When you can say the same, then you can stand in judgment of me."

I sat there in total shock with tears pouring down

my face. That was the first time she had ever laid a hand on me. Without saying a single word, I stood up from the table, grabbed my coat, and headed for the door. By this time she was crying too. I'm sure she was as stunned as I was by what had happened. As I walked out the door, she tried to apologize. "I'm sorry Karen, I just want you to be happy." I looked back at her barely able to speak and mumbled, "That's exactly what I've been trying to tell you for years."

During the twenty minute ride home, I reflected back on what my mother said. But no matter how hard I tried to make sense of it, I couldn't. There was no way in hell I was going to spend the rest of my life sharing my husband, and seven years of marriage and two kids didn't mean a damn thing to me. I wanted love and trust out of my relationship, and I wasn't getting either. "This must all end," I declared. "I'm sick and tired of waiting, worrying, and crying over this man." It was time to stop playing the fool. After wiping my face and blowing my runny nose, I decided the next time he slipped up would be his last. All I needed was one tiny reason to explode. That opportunity came two weeks later during the fourth of July barbecue at my mom's house.

I hadn't spoken to my mother since the incident took place. When Jason and I arrived with the kids, she quickly ushered me aside and apologized for everything that happened. Like most women, we got all sentimental and started crying. I'm sure everyone was wondering what all the drama was about, but this was strictly between mother and daughter. Once the entire family was there, we sat down to eat. As usual, the food was outstanding. My mother really knows how to put her foot in some collard greens and potato salad.

After everyone was full, the family split into three groups. The kids went outside, the women gathered in the living room, and the men flocked to the basement. It wasn't long before Carolyn and Aunt Dorothy went into their act about no good men. Needless to say, I wasn't in the mood, so I went into the kitchen to refill my drink. Right away I noticed the door to the basement was wide open. As I went to close it, I could hear my drunk brother and husband boasting loudly about their sexual escapades. I just stood there and took it all in.

"Man, it's impossible for any man to be right with so many temptations out there." my brother asserted.

"Who are you tellin'?" Jason emphatically agreed. "Just last week a woman came into the office wearing a skirt so short half her ass was showing."

"Did you inform her that her attire was inappropriate for corporate America?"

"Hell no, I complimented her on the outfit and asked for her phone number."

The room exploded with laughter. I could hear the customary high fives and foot stomping. But they weren't through putting their feet in their mouths.

"What about the sex drives some of these young women have?" My horny 45 year old Uncle Frank joked. "This 23 year old filly I just met damn near threw my back out at the motel last night."

"Well at least she's working hard to please her man," Jason said. "That's one thing I can honestly say about these other women, they serve you better than your own wife."

That was the straw that broke the camel's back. I slammed my glass on the counter and rushed downstairs with smoke coming out my ears.

"You all have a lot of damn nerve bragging about your whores right under the same roof as your wives. I have never seen such disrespect. Daddy you should be ashamed. And as for you Jason, let me educate you about real life before I divorce your no good ass. Sex at home has responsibility. I have two kids to raise, a house to clean, and a lazy man to clean up after. Not to mention school and work."

"Hold on baby, let me explain."

"Shut the hell up, I'm not finished yet!" I shouted. "And if you would have just once offered to cook breakfast or take care of the kids for just one morning, I would have given you the fuck of your life, but no. You preferred to rush out of the house to do your business elsewhere, fine. From now on let your part time slut take on some full time responsibility and let's see how desirable she is in six months."

I ran upstairs, told my mother I was leaving, and got my kids together. Jason tried to stop me but one look into my eyes and he could see I was on the verge of seriously going off. He wisely took his ass back into the house while my mother helped me to the car. Once the kids were strapped in and I was preparing to pull off, she suddenly reached inside the car and gave me a firm hug. "You were right baby," she confessed. "You do deserve better. Call me if you need help getting settled." I kissed her goodbye and drove away with my two kids to start a new life. As I headed for home, confident that I had made the right decision, I looked in the rear view mirror at my kids playing in the back seat. I swore right then and there to teach them to take marriage and commitment more seriously than their father did. I promised to raise my son to cherish and respect women. And as for my daughter, I vowed not to create another victim, so help me God.

For many women in our society, leaving their cheating husbands and boyfriends is not an option. Again, they are too afraid of being alone to seriously confront him and issue an ultimatum—"Either stop fooling around or it's over between us." This is the warning which should be coming out of the mouths of fed up women, but doesn't. Instead they remain quiet, hoping and praying their man will grow up or slow down long enough to realize he has a good thing at home. However, most men are convinced the grass is greener on the other side of town, at least green enough to go grazing in once or twice a week. They have become bored conversationally and sexually with their mates and feel compelled to seek satisfaction elsewhere. "I need a change," they declare. But the person who really needs a change is the faithful wife or girlfriend, a change of men to be exact.

And it is this issue of change itself which is at the heart of many failed relationships. The woman is looking forward to it, while the man is fighting against it. "I'll be your husband or boyfriend," the man thinks, "but my lifestyle isn't going to change." Meanwhile, the infatuated woman is presuming, "Once we get together everything will change." For whatever reason women are under the impression that just because a man says, "I do," that all of his desires to be with other women will magically disappear. How ridiculous. Men who cheat before getting married, or engaged, will cheat afterwards, it's that simple. And all of the good conversation, good cooking, and good pussy in the world isn't going to stop them.

But don't try to tell that to the hard-headed woman of the 90s, who is determined to solve every riddle, heal every wound, and right every wrong. She utterly refuses to accept the fact that her man cannot or will not commit. "Why is that?" you ask. I believe it has a great deal to do with the woman's instinctual need to nurture and pamper. For some strange reason she perceives infidelity as an emotional disease which can be remedied with a little patience and her overwhelming love. "He just hasn't found the right woman," she declares. However, the reality is that he has found the perfect woman, one who will stand idly by and keep her mouth shut while he does his business.

Like a moth to the flame, burned by the fire, 35 year old Denise also fell in love with a cheating man who would inevitably violate her trust and break her heart. When she first met her boyfriend Kevin, the challenge of changing him seemed very exciting. But as the years rolled by and his cheating persisted, the magnetic lights grew dim and the attraction faded. "My pampering and rehabilitation days are over," she declares. "I need a real man who has made up his own mind to be faithful, not some immature jerk who needs to be watched over like a damned baby." Clearly, she has had quite enough of the hand holding and game playing. With the support of her girlfriends, who were also fed up with the infidelity in their own relationships, she finally woke up and put her foot down. Well, it's about time!

> Sometimes I look in the mirror and ask myself, "Denise how could you have been so stupid?" For years I was in love with a man who seemed more like a spoiled child than a boyfriend. Instead of holding him responsible for his actions, I made excuses for everything he did wrong. When he came over with lipstick on his collar, I ignored it telling myself, "It's nothing, don't make a scene." The time he accidentally called me by another woman's name, I had a logical explanation,

"That's probably the name of one of his co-workers." And when he couldn't get it up in bed, I was right there with his defense. "He's just tired from working overtime." Boy, was I ever right about that one.

My relationship with Kevin lasted three long and painful years. During which time he must have dumped me on at least six different occasions. He would conveniently start a fight over something stupid just to get away to spend the holiday or weekend with his whore. And just like a fool, I would be right there waiting when he was ready to patch things up. The last time this happened was about a year ago. I can't even remember what it was about. When the argument was over he was storming out of the door, swearing it was over between us for good. I didn't know at the time, but he was right. However, this time it was going to be over on my terms.

There I was, on yet another Saturday afternoon, alone. As usual I was crying and totally pissed with Kevin for the one millionth time. I decided to call my girlfriends April and Monica. "If nothing else, I can curse his ass out and get an Amen," I thought. And God knows those were two women who would co-sign on anything negative said about a no good, two timing, dirty dog. April's husband Tony worked for the post office, and Monica's boyfriend Raymond was a Police officer, both of whom were fooling around on the side. By the way, Kevin worked for the Chicago Transit Authority as a train conductor, talk about three whorish occupations. As I dialed April's number, I tried to gain my composure, but the minute I heard her voice, the tears started pouring again.

"Hello?" April's voice inquired.

"Hello, April, it's me," I sobbed.

"Denise is that you? What's wrong girl? Don't tell me, it's Kevin again, isn't it?"

"You know it. We just had another argument and he broke things off, again."

"Well, good riddance. You should be celebrating and not crying," she said with an attitude. "Those damn CTA men are the biggest whores in town."

"You're right, but look who's talking," I said trying to lighten things up. "You were crying on my shoulder like a baby last week when you found a condom in Tony's wallet. I guess he's been delivering more than the mail lately."

"Awe, so now you want to crack on me, huh?" she said as we both laughed. "Hold on while I call Monica and put her on the three way."

It never took very long for me to snap out of my misery when I talked to my girls. We took turns cheering each other up when things got rough, sort of like a battered woman's group. Lately, it seemed the support was needed more than ever. As I wiped my face with a towel, April clicked back over with Monica on the line.

"Hey baby girl, you all right?" Monica asked in a motherly tone.

"Yeah, I'll be fine. I just need time to chill out."

"Well good, now let me tell you about what Raymond tried to pull on me yesterday," she said out of nowhere.

"Dag Monica, we haven't even dealt with Denise's problem yet," April said.

"No April, let her go on. Maybe listening to someone else's problems will do me some good," I said jokingly.

"Ok, check this out. You know Raymond was supposed to have a patrol assignment at Chicago Stadium, right?"

"Right," April and I said in unison.

"Well, I went by his house to drop off his birthday card because I couldn't find the one I wanted soon enough to mail it on time. Anyway, when I drove up, I saw him and another woman coming out the door. They were both in civilian clothes and holding hands."

"You've got to be kidding girl," April said sounding totally shocked.

"Wait, that's not the good part. Can you believe he had the nerve to tell me she was his assigned partner, and they were working undercover?"

"They were working undercover all right," I said. "Under his bed covers."

"Then what happened?" April asked. "Did you maintain your ladylike composure?"

"Well of course I did. I politely threw the card in his face, called her a bitch, and drove off."

"It must be something in the water," I laughed. "First April finds a condom in Tony's wallet, then Kevin dumps me for no reason, now you bust Raymond in the act, what a week."

"Wait a minute April," Monica interjected. "You went through Kevin's wallet?"

"You damn right I did. It was lying right out in the open."

"Out in the open?" Monica asked. "Exactly what do you consider out in the open?"

"At the bottom of his dresser drawer, under my roof."

"Well baby, let me tell you. Once you start going through a man's belongings, you're already out of control and on your way to divorce court."

"Whatever, Monica. All I know is he better get his act together, or my daughter and I will be flying the friendly skies without him."

April is a 28-year-old flight attendant, and very attractive. I really couldn't understand why Tony was cheating on her. Any man would've been happy to be in his shoes, and in his bed. Now, Monica was the mother hen of the group. She is 37 years old, well educated, with a body and a walk that could stop traffic. Again, I couldn't understand why Raymond was tripin'. Monica was a class act who could pick and choose any man she wanted. But she loved Raymond's dirty drawers and he probably knew it. As for me, I've been told I have it going on, too. Although I may be slightly overweight, some men insist on having a woman with a little meat on her bones. Kevin just didn't know how good he had it.

So why were we putting up with these three knuckleheads? you ask. The answer to that question was the topic of conversation at dinner that evening. We decided to treat ourselves to a nice meal, and then go out to the club to release some of our frustration, and burn off a few calories. April had to rush to find a babysitter, Monica was determined to get her hair done, and I wanted to go over to Woman's Workout World to get a little exercise in. It was 5:00 when we finally got off the phone. The plan was to meet at the restaurant downtown at 8:00, and I had every intention of being on time and dressed to kill.

The moment I returned from the gym, I pulled my sharpest outfit and 3 inch pumps out of the closet. I was determined to squeeze my wide ass into that tight dress, with or without Crisco. Fortunately for me, twenty minutes on the stairmaster, and thirty minutes in the sauna did the trick. After taking my shower, and oiling down my body, I slid into that dress with no problem at all. Next I put on my make up and painted my nails. As I looked in the mirror at the finished product, I saw a confident, voluptuous, full figured woman who had been deprived of a good man and good lovin' for far too long. Not once in three years had Kevin ever taken me out to a nice restaurant and then dancing. It's like he was ashamed of being seen in public with me. "But that's all right though," I proudly said to myself. "Never ask a boy to do a man sized job."

It was 7:30 before I stopped admiring myself and decided to leave. Once in my car, I turned the rear view mirror towards myself and confessed, "April and Monica may only be going out to unwind, but I'm on the hunt tonight. And what a night it turned out to be.

To my surprise April and Monica were waiting at the bar when I arrived at the restaurant. They were sitting with their backs towards me surrounded by men, so I couldn't see what they were wearing. "Please God, don't let them be dressed too conservatively," I thought. What a waste of a prayer that was. When they stood up from their stools and turned around to greet me, I damn near fell out. April's fast behind had on lace stockings and a strapless mini dress that barely covered her ass. Tony would have killed her if he saw her in that outfit. Monica was sharp as usual. Her 5′ 10″ frame made her look like a fashion model. She was wearing a black halter dress with a push up bra underneath that made her 32 B's look like 36 D's.

Needless to say, we didn't pay for any drinks that evening. As a matter of fact, we didn't pay for dinner either. When the waitress came over to take our order, she told us it was on the house. The manager, who was fresh on Monica, flipped the bill. All he wanted in return was a minute of her time before dinner and her phone number. I was ready to give it to him myself. Since he was a little cute and we were a lot broke, she went along with his request. But the second the food arrived, she cut him off and came over to eat.

"Well, that's that," she nonchalantly said. "Dig in, it's on me."

"You are cold-blooded, Monica," April said. "You have no intention of calling him, do you?"

"Of course not. Hey, I didn't ask him to spend his money. I can't help it if men like to show off with their wallets. And besides, they throw out tons of food every night anyway. He's just trying to impress me, but I'm not easily impressed."

Monica always had deep words of wisdom, except when it came to explaining why she was putting up with Raymond. I had always been curious as to why women as beautiful as they were put up with men who treat them so bad. No doubt, they were probably wondering the same about me. Well, it didn't take long before all the free drinks began to loosen our inhibitions and our tongues, especially mine.

"Monica, you mind if I ask you a personal question?"

"No, go right ahead."

"Why do you put up with Raymond's B.S. when you could have any man you want."

"To be honest with you Denise, sometimes I don't know myself. I guess I don't have the patience to train another man. Raymond may be a dog, but he's predictable."

"That's so unfair," April asserted. "Men can sleep around with all the women they want, but let a man look sideways at their wife or girlfriend and all hell would break loose."

"That's because men know they have women right where they want them, especially black men," I said. "I recently read a study which stated 70% of black males would be unavailable by the year 2000."

"Unavailable meaning what?" April asked.

"Unavailable to the heterosexual black female for a relationship, that's what."

"To hell with the year 2000, they're unavailable now," Monica laughed. "Either they're locked up, doped up, unemployed, under employed, married, homosexual, or just too damned ugly to look at."

April was so amused that she almost spit her drink out. Her face got red, and tears started streaming down the side of her face, she was cracking up. For a minute I thought she was choking to death, but she was alright.

"Girl, are you trying to kill me?" April said after composing herself. "Don't ever say anything that funny while I'm trying to swallow."

"But it's the truth, and you both know it. Look at our men for example. All of them are good looking, have well paying jobs, and are surrounded by hundreds of skeezers everyday. And you know they're the biggest skeezer pleasers in town."

"You may be right, but I know how to put Tony's ass in check." April said.

"And how's that, may I ask?"

"I'll just go on strike. No cooking, no laundry, and definitely no pussy."

"Well, I've got my own methods for getting Raymond to behave. My Jamaican friend at work taught me a little voodoo. She told me to get one of his pictures, cut the head off, and place it face up in the crotch of my panties."

"And what's that supposed to do?" I asked.

"I don't exactly know, but the first two weeks I tried it, Raymond was wearing my thighs like ear muffs every morning."

"Stop fooling around Monica, this is serious," I said.

"Ok then, why have you put up with old buck tooth, big nose, two timing Kevin for the last three years? He must have a gold plated dick to keep you coming back after all the hell he's put you through."

"With me, I think it's a matter of how I feel about myself. Kevin has been telling me for so long that nobody else would ever want me, that I actually started believing him. When we first met, he would compliment me on my figure and my outfits. Now, all of a sudden I'm dressing whorish and getting too fat. I think he's just trying to lower my self-esteem so he can control me."

"Ok, that's enough of this depressing conversation," Monica said as she reached inside her purse. "I've got something for you to read and then we're out of here."

"What is it?" April asked.

"It's an office joke being faxed around town."

She pulled out two pieces of paper with large typing on it and handed it to us, it read:

MENopause
MENstrual cramps
MENtal illness
MENtal breakdown

Ever notice how all our problems begin with men?

After getting a good laugh and a spirit boost, we freshened up and were on our way. It was 10:00 and way past all our bed times, but the conversation and the alcohol had us hyped. As we drove the few blocks to the club side by side, I rolled down my window and rowdily shouted, "Lookout men, here we come!"

It had been several months since any of us had been out on the club scene. The music sounded louder and the men were more attractive than I remembered. We tried our best not to look uncomfortable or unfamiliar with the surroundings. Men can sniff out new meat like blood hounds. As we strutted past all the jealous looks and turned up noses, it was obvious things hadn't changed much. Women still spend most of their time checking out each other. After finding a table and getting ourselves situated, we began scoping the place out for good prospects. Right away I saw a gentleman who was just my type. Tall, dark, and most importantly, alone. When I tried to make a seductive gesture to get his attention, the guy next to him thought I was flirting with him.

"I saw that," Monica said. "You got the wrong one, didn't you?"

"Damn, and here he comes," I said under my breath. Like a snake crawling out from under a rock this Jerry curl wearing thug slithered through the crowd towards our table. I turned my back to discourage his approach, but it was too late.

"Excuse me Ms. Lady," he said while tapping me on shoulder. "My name is Lenny."

"Hi Lenny," I said trying not to choke from the smell of the chemicals in his hair and his cheap cologne.

"Can I buy you a drink?" he asked.

"No thank you, I'm waiting for my boyfriend."

"Well baby, if you change your mind, remember I'm Lenny and I've got plenty."

As he walked away he looked back and smiled at me with that annoying gold tooth protruding halfway out of his mouth. April busted him out the minute he was out of hearing distance.

"Hell naw, no he didn't say he was Lenny with plenty. He needs to quit with his countrified, fake Billy Dee Williams lookin' ass."

Monica was bent over in her chair crackin' up. She had to put both hands over her mouth to keep from laughing in his face. And who could blame her? Some of the raps you hear are so weak you've got to laugh to keep from crying.

"Lord, I need a drink," Monica said as she wiped her face with kleenex.

No sooner did she say that did the waitress arrive at the table with anonymous drink offers. We all accepted and ordered our usual, double shots of cognac. After receiving the drinks, we sat up straight in our stools and waited for the man or men who paid the tab to make the next move.

"Whoever paid for this Martel better get over here in a hurry," April said.

"Why is that?" I asked.

"Because this drink is like an hour glass, once it's empty, his time is up."

Right on cue, two fine looking men walked up to the table. One of them was light skinned, with a stocky build. And the other, who just happened to be the man I was trying to flirt with earlier, was slim with hazel eyes and tight buns. Mmm Mmm good.

"Hello ladies," the slim one said. "My name is Lawrence, this is my partner Dexter, mind if we join you?"

"Hell no! I mean, be my guest," I enthusiastically, but cordially responded. "My name is Denise, this is April, and the tall beautiful one over there is Monica."

"I hope you're enjoying your drink," Dexter said as he purposely looked in April's direction.

"Yes, I am. Thank you very much."

"What about you, Denise?" Lawrence flirtatiously inquired.

"You're fine, I mean it's fine, thank you."

It didn't take long to tell that April and I had been chosen. Monica was the odd man out this time, which didn't happen all that often. Not surprisingly, she took the opportunity to make light of the situation.

"So what am I some kind of charity case?" Monica joked.

"Oh no sweetheart, that's not it at all. I just figured a woman with your height would prefer a taller man," Lawrence apologetically explained.

"You're right about that, sweetheart. So, do you have any friends who are 6´ 5″ and over?"

"As a matter of fact I do, but unfortunately they're not here tonight."

"Oh well, be sure to tell them what they missed."

Monica was ready to party, but nobody would ask her to dance. The men were obviously intimidated by her beauty and size. For some strange reason, it seemed as if all the men were under six feet that night. April joked with her saying, "Didn't you know this was 6 ft and under get in free night?" Finally, after several good songs played, a cute guy who was about 5´ 2″ asked her to dance. At that point, all she needed was an escort out onto the floor, after that he could drop dead. The minute she hit the floor, she started showing off. Her nieces had just taught her how to do a new dance called the Percolator and she was giving lessons. Oh yes, Monica could dance her ass off.

April and I were waiting for the DJ to play a Steppers song. We were completely out of practice on the latest dances, but Steppin' was smooth and simple. It's like riding a bike, once you learn, you never forget. For those of you who don't know what Steppin' is, ask someone from Chicago or the Midwest. In some cities it's called Bopping. In others, it's known as hand dancing. But nobody does it better then we do here in Chitown, nobody. As I was saying, we were too far behind the latest dances to go out there and embarrass ourselves, but that didn't stop Monica. She was having a ball and showing her age. While the entire crowd was swaying back and forth to the rhythm shouting, "Hey, Ho, Hey Ho," Monica's old ass was yelling, "The roof, the roof, the roof is on fire." It was apparent that she was a little tipsy and out of party practice.

Finally, after what seemed like forever, the DJ played a couple of Steppin' records, Summer Madness and the cut Mind Blow Decisions by Heatwave. We quickly assigned Monica to purse watching duty and slid onto the floor. April and I were shocked to discover that both Dexter and Lawrence could really throw down. They were shuffling and turning so precisely you would have sworn they practiced all their moves together. I was impressed, and so was April. When the songs ended, we returned to the table laughing and joking like old friends, I was really having a great time. For the next two hours we were pampered and flattered more than we had been in years. Kevin, Tony, and Raymond were distant memories, or so I thought.

I didn't notice right away, but Monica was running back and forth to the bathroom every ten to fifteen minutes. I just figured she either had a weak bladder or was checking somebody out. Then it dawned on me, she was making a booty call to Raymond, I was sure of it. "Why else is she peeking inside her purse to see if anyone is paging her at 1:00 a.m?" I thought to myself. My suspicions were confirmed when she pulled me aside and told me she had to leave.

"Denise I hate to be a party pooper, but I've got to go."

"I don't believe you Monica," I said with disappointment. "You just caught Raymond fucking somebody yesterday and you're running back to him today, and at 1:00 in the morning."

"You don't understand girlfriend, Raymond just needs his space every now and then. And just like I told you, I've invested too much time into training him."

"You're the one who's trained Monica, or should I say dick whipped?"

"Look, I don't have time for this right now, tell April I'll talk to her later, bye."

She kissed me on the cheek and shot out the door like her house was on fire, or should I say her pussy? All I could do was shake my head while walking back to the table. For the very first time, I realized just how pitiful I must have sounded trying to defend Kevin all those years. This was too deep. My mind was reeling, "How do women allow themselves to become so blind?" I thought. Needless to say, my night was ruined. I asked

Lawrence for his number, gave him a hug, and went home with plenty to think about. April was enjoying herself and decided to stay awhile longer. She was flying out of town the next afternoon and wanted to make the most of it. I didn't blame her one bit. Dexter was cute, fun to be around, and a perfect gentleman.

First thing Monday morning, I called my job and requested a week's vacation. During the next few days, I didn't talk to anyone. I switched on my answering machine and turned down the volume. I needed time for myself. Every morning at 7:00 a.m., I got up and went to the gym for a light workout and swim. I even treated myself to a nice dinner a few nights just to celebrate being me. But what I enjoyed most was taking steamy hot bubble baths by candlelight. Yes, I was really beginning to feel good about myself. For the first time in a long time, I made myself top priority. By Friday afternoon, I was ready to return my calls, which had piled up considerably over the last five days. I quickly fast forwarded past the bill collectors and telemarketers. The remaining messages were truly shocking.

(Beep) "Denise, this is Monica," she said sounding depressed. "I just got back from seeing my doctor. He told me I had chlamydia. I'm too old for this shit, Raymond has got to go. Please call me as soon as possible, bye."

(Beep) "Denise if you're there pick up, this is April. Oh well, I guess you've heard the bad news by now. Poor Monica, when will she ever learn? Anyway, I have some great news myself. I'm flying to Nassau for the weekend. No, not with Tony. I'm going with Dexter Saint Jock," she laughed. "I had a couple of tickets lying around that my neglectful husband was too busy to use.

Now, I know what you're thinking, two wrongs don't make a right. Well, it may not make it right but it damn sure makes it even. Call you when I get back, bye."

Before she hung up, I could here a Bob Marley song playing in the background, "I shot the sheriff." April was on cloud nine and I couldn't have been happier for her. She deserved all the love and attention she could get. Too bad Monica didn't wake up before she got burned. Anyway, there was still one final message to retrieve. One that would test my self-respect and my resolve.

(Beep) "Denise this is Kevin. I just called to tell you I'm sorry. I know I haven't been right lately, but I miss you baby. Give me a call so we can work things out. I'll be waiting, love you."

Boy, I hated when he did that. Every time we broke up, he tried to sweet talk me into forgiving him. And like a fool, I fell for it each and every time. I told myself over and over again, "Not this time Denise. Don't let your heart sell out your brain." I didn't know what to do. "Should I call?" I contemplated. "Or should I just let things fade?" I decided to think it over for another day. Besides, Monica had provided me with enough drama for one day. When I called her later that evening, she had already confronted Raymond about the STD and accepted his apology for slipping up, as he put it. There was no point in wasting my time dogging him. Her nose was wide open and he could do no wrong. After giving her my two cents worth of advice, I turned my attention to how I was going to respond to Kevin's apology.

When I woke up Saturday morning, I decided not to bother calling Kevin. I figured I'd leave him hanging the way he had done me on so many occasions. With that settled, I went about my routine of working out and relaxing. I felt like a new woman. My mind was at peace and my confidence level was high. All I needed was someone to talk to, not Monica or April either. I needed to hear a man's voice. Yes, Lawrence was definitely on my mind, but I wasn't ready to get deep in another relationship so soon. He made it perfectly clear he wanted more than a friendship. As he put it, "I'm not interested in being some woman's girlfriend with a penis. Either you're sexually attracted to me or you aren't." At the time I was offended, and a bit disappointed with his attitude. I assumed he only wanted to sleep around with every woman he met, but I was wrong. What I believe he was trying to get across was, "My time is valuable and I prefer to spend it with a woman who is interested in having an intimate relationship with me." At the very least, I should have respected his honesty, which I do now.

By night fall, I was curled up on my leather sofa listening to V-103 on the radio. The dusties were sounding great and a cool breeze was blowing through the patio window. I was feeling so good that I decided to break out my six month old bottle of Beringer wine and get drunk while reading Terry McMillan's, "Waiting to Exhale." And just when I was getting to the good part where Bernardine set her husband's BMW on fire, the phone rang. Without thinking, I instinctively picked it up. What a mistake that turned out to be, it was Kevin.

"What's up baby, why didn't you return my call?" he said trying to sound hard.

"I've been busy," I replied with an attitude.

"Well, can we talk?"

"I don't have anything to say. You're the one who dumped me, remember?"

"Yeah, I know, and I'm sorry."

"You're sorry alright. Sorry and tired!"

"Don't be like that baby, you know how much I care about you."

"If this is how you treat someone you care about, I can do without it. And stop calling me baby, I'm a grown woman, and it's about time you found that out."

At that very moment, an old song by The Jones Girls came on the radio, "You Gonna Make Me Love Somebody Else." I stopped listening to Kevin's begging, sat the phone on my lap, and tuned into the song. The opening lyrics said it all.

You gonna make me love somebody else, if you keep on treating me the way you do.

I ain't did nothin' to you. I just loved you with my heart and soul.

Every time I need some lovin', why do you turn cold, turn cold?

Now, I ain't dumb and I ain't stupid, I know you need love like I do.

Cause if you ain't lovin' me, I wanna know who in the world you lovin'? Tell me if you don't want me around.

"Amen to that!" I shouted. "These sisters must have made that song especially for me." When I picked up the phone, Kevin was still begging and going on about how much he loved me.

"Denise, you know I love you baby. Nobody will ever love you the way I do," he professed. "Don't you still love me?"

I paused, took a deep breath, and thought about all of the hell he put me through over the years. And in a calm and convincing tone I responded.

"You must have the wrong number, love don't live here anymore," and hung up.

AFTERWORD

In the ruthless game of cheating there are no romantic conclusions or happy endings, only rude awakenings and hard lessons. Lessons which I hope men and women will apply to their own relationships to help build them up and not break them down. Once the problem areas have been identified, they are much simpler to deal with and resolve. But beware, infidelity is not a feeble condition which simply fades away like a headache or the common cold. It is a potent disease which will resurface over and over again until someone puts an end to it, once and for all. And those women who are involved in these relationships, whether it be as wives or mistresses, have the power to do just that. They must, in the strongest terms, demand to be treated with respect and honesty. No woman should willingly remain in a situation where her happiness and dignity is selfishly compromised. If men can belligerently insist on absolute loyalty, then so can women. Likewise, men have a responsibility to lift themselves above their egotistical and animalistic cravings for sexual and emotional conquests. They must learn to deal honestly with the women in their lives and communicate their preference for an open relationship. Women have a right to be given a choice based on the truth.

As for me, I have grown weary of the cheating game. It is an emotionally draining and non-productive indulgence which requires constant lying and more lying. Multiple lies create stress, stress affects clear thinking, and the lack of clear thinking impairs creativity. Like most men who are serious about getting ahead, I prefer to utilize my valuable time and God given talent on something more constructive than maneuvering women into bed, like writing this book for example. The accomplishment of a worthwhile goal is much more exhilarating and financially rewarding than any orgasm. However, the most significant reason why I no longer view cheating as an option is because of all the unnecessary pain it has caused so many innocent women throughout my life. Women who only wanted to love and be loved unconditionally. I'm sick and tired of living with the guilty feelings of breaking hearts and causing tears to be shed. There comes a time in every man's life when he must stop making empty promises just to take advantage of women. That time for me is now. I vow that the next time a woman sheds tears over me, they will be tears of joy, not pain.

LOVE, LUST, & LIES

Relationship Video

This provocative relationship video is a collection of Michael's entertaining and thought-provoking seminars.

He addresses issues such as infidelity, the conniving other woman, and frustrating dating games. It's a great conversation piece for book clubs, bachelor parties, and other get-togethers.

Order your copy today!

Call **1-800-772-0524** *(orders only)*

To order books or tapes online, log on to
www.lovelustlies.com

Men Cry In The Dark

Another best-seller by Michael Baisden

The bad boy of literature is back! Michael is taking the book world by storm once again with a provocative book that is sure to stir controversy. *Men Cry In The Dark* is an entertaining and realistic novel about relationships, fatherhood, and interracial dating from the man's perspective. And in an industry dominated by female writers, it's long overdue!

Men Cry In The Dark has been called the male's version of *Waiting to Exhale*. The story centers around four men and how they deal with their relationships, but that's where the similarities end. Michael's characters are strong successful men who live in two worlds, the world of big business and the streets. Like many men who have made it out of the inner-city ghettos, his characters, Derrick, Tony, Ben, and Mark, represent the thousands of men who struggle with the challenges of their professional lives while trying not to forget where they come from. Never before has a book tackled so many controversial social and relationship issues: fatherhood, gold-diggers, and interracial dating. It has all the makings of another best-seller, and hopefully a major motion picture. Michael says, "It's *Boomerang*, *Love Jones,* and *Boyz N the Hood,* all rolled into one."

For more information about book signing dates and to subscribe to our newsletter, log on to our Web site at

www.lovelustlies.com

You can also purchase books and tapes for 20% to 30% off retail.

To order by phone, call **1-800-772-0524** *(orders only).*

The Maintenance Man

RECENT RELEASE by Michael Baisden

The Maintenance Man is an intriguing novel about love, betrayal, and of course, sex. Michael paints a dark picture of his main character, Malcolm, who is a high-priced gigolo struggling with his morality. He is conflicted with his promiscuous lifestyle and his desire to pursue his dream as a pianist. While on an appointment with one of his wealthy clients, he meets a beautiful and gifted dancer named Antoinette, Toni for short. She recognizes his incredible talent and encourages him to go after his dream. But Toni is unaware of Malcolm's unsavory occupation. And trying to keep it undercover only adds to the drama.

Meanwhile, Malcolm's best friend, Simon, is dealing with his own issues. His fianceé, Cynthia is creeping with the local preacher. But Simon is so busy running the hottest spot in Atlanta, Club Obsession, that he doesn't notice the change until it's too late. But once he discovers the betrayal, all hell breaks loose. Simon finds comfort with his attractive young manager, Ariel, who offers what little support she can.

However, Ariel has her own problems as she struggles with being childless and single at age thirty. She becomes so desperate that she calls the radio station hook-up line. But instead of finding the man of her dreams, she runs into a series of nightmares. If you love to hate a character, than Theodore a.k.a. Teddy Bear, is your man. He is a manipulating player and dead beat dad. He works at Club Obsession on Ladies' Night as the star stripper, a job he uses to his advantage to attract lonely and desperate women to take care of him. While they scream and stuff his thong with twenty dollar bills, he's scheming on how he can take them for every dime they've got.

ABOUT THE AUTHOR

Michael Baisden was born June 26, 1963, in Chicago, Illinois. After two years of college he joined the Air Force where he continued his education and became interested in literature. "Terry McMillan, Ralph Ellison, Napoleon Hill, and Jawanza Kunjufu were among my favorites," he says. "But I felt there was a void in the book industry." There were very few authors writing about relationships from the man's perspective." After being honorably discharged in 1988, he established Legacy, Inc., a company specializing in the manufacture of leather products. But it wasn't until 1993 that he discovered his God-given talent was writing. In January 1995, he self-published his first book, *Never Satisfied: How & Why Men Cheat*, and his life hasn't been the same since.

Michael has established himself as one of the top authors in the country today. His electrifying personality has earned him repeated appearances on talk shows such as *Ricki Lake*, *Maury Povich*, *Sally Jesse*, *Maureen O'Boyle*, *The View*, *Rolonda*, and *BET Tonight with Tavis Smiley*. Michael is also a charismatic speaker. He has performed in front of standing-room-only audiences at events all across the country. His relationship seminars have toured cities such as Philadelphia, Boston, Dallas, Houston, Charlotte, Chicago, St. Louis, Los Angeles, San Francisco, Oakland, Washington, Atlanta, and Cleveland, just to name a few. And each time the audiences were left speechless and enlightened by his candid style.

For more information about when the *Love, Lust, and Lies* seminar is coming to a city near you, log on to Legacy Publishing's web site at
www.michaelbaisden.com
Or you may send a brief letter to request information on how to schedule a seminar for your organization, convention, or exposition to:

Legacy Publishing
PO Box 6555
Katy, TX 77491-6555

Or send e-mail to **mb@michaelbaisden.com**

Note to all bookclubs: Please e-mail your web address *or* write to the above address.